Chesapeake's Bounty

Katie Moose

Conduit Press
Easton, Maryland

Katie Moose, born in Baltimore, is a descendant of the Clagett (Claggett) family of Maryland, and many old New England whaling families. She has lived in many of the U.S.' great architectural, historical and waterside gems besides Easton – Annapolis, MD; New Castle, DE; Newport and Providence, RI; Cold Spring Harbor, NY; San Francisco; Philadelphia; Greenwich, CT; Alexandria, VA; Washington, DC; and New York City. She and her family also maintain homes on historic Nantucket Island.

Mrs. Moose was the co-author of "The Best of Newport"; and is the author of "Annapolis: The Guidebook", "Eastern Shore of Maryland: The Guidebook", Chesapeake's Bounty II, New England's Bounty, "Nantucket's Bounty"; and Maryland's Western Shore: The Guidebook"

Conduit Press wishes to thank Mount Clare Mansion, Baltimore, Maryland and the National Society of Colonial Dames of America in the State of Maryland for permission to use photographs of the house.

Front cover design: Jean Harper Baer, Baltimore, Maryland
Pictures on pages 1, 47, 109, 129, 144, 159 were photographed by George H. Moose, Jr. and used with his permission.

Copyright ©2000   Conduit Press
1st Printing 2000
2nd Printing 2000
3rd Printing 2005
4th Printing 2007

Published by Conduit Press, 307 Goldsborough Street, Easton, Maryland 21601

Library of Congress Cataloging-in-Publication Data

Printed and Bound by United Book Press, Baltimore, Maryland

ISBN: 978-0-9666610-3-6

COOKBOOK TABLE OF CONTENTS

PICTURES

"We may live without poetry, music and art;
We may live without conscience, and live without heart
We may live without friends; we may live without books;
But civilized man cannot live without cooks."
Edward Robert Bulwer-Lytton, Earl of Lytton (1831-91)

Sunrise - Eastern Shore of Maryland

"Cookery is become an art, a noble science;
cooks are gentlemen"
Robert Burton (1577-1640)

INTRODUCTION

The bounty of the Chesapeake Bay region equals few other regions of the world with its abundance of seafood, poultry, fresh vegetables and fruits. The Chesapeake is the largest bay in the United States.

For several years my grandfather, Grafton Sherwood Kennedy was stationed at Aberdeen Proving Grounds as Chief of Staff to my Godfather, Major General Alfred Bixby Quinton. He was posted there two other times. My grandparents later retired to "Harmony Hills Farm" in Darlington. Following World War II my parents lived at "Mount Pleasant" in Havre de Grace and after my birth stayed on for almost a year. The next ten years were spent in New Castle, Delaware, which is where we met Auntie Phyl whose mouthwatering "Utterly Deadly Southern Pecan Pie" is included. I remember those summer days when my mother spent many hours canning or freezing the plentiful fresh vegetables and fruits, or going to the Seabrook outlet just across the river in New Jersey. There was no Delaware Memorial Bridge back then

My mother had grown up in a household with help and the only time she was allowed in the kitchen was to lick the bowl. She was determined all three of her children would learn how to cook properly. Today my sister has a successful catering business in Lake Forest, Illinois and my brother can come up with a perfect coffee cake or venison stroganoff. My mother has kept my father fed for 60 plus years!

Since the early 1970s while living in San Francisco, I have wanted to write a cookbook. Several of us would gather together and plan a whole menu from Gourmet Magazine or come up with our own. The Junior League also had a gourmet dinner group in which two ladies would plan and execute the menu, every other month, rotating through the group. I'll never forget the first time I had "duty". What seemed like an easy menu finally involved our husbands getting it to the table on time.

At the time my daughter was born we lived in Alexandria, Virginia. From my daughter's earliest years she loved certain recipes, and could help me take a recipe and turn it into something very special. The first one I remember was the Fourth of July pie she created on Nantucket during one of our many vacations there. Today she is a chef in Cleveland and practices what she has enjoyed these many years.

Later living in Cleveland, I had the pleasure of being a part of a family of cooks and wine experts. I quickly learned that it was best for me to cook. When the brothers arrived they knew how to use every pot, bowl and utensil, and you know who had to pick up afterwards. I taught myself many shortcuts and they all seemed to work, even now.

Today we reside in the historic and beautiful city of Annapolis, keeping our boats on the Eastern Shore. My husband learned some of his most favorite recipes from Loretta Larrimore, wife of skipjack captain Stanley Larrimore while living on Tilghman Island, and later watching the cooking shows on TV. Though his family is not from this area, we have included recipes from "Now Let Us Praise Fried Pies" compiled by George's cousin Ryland Swain of Washington for the Hall-Lay family reunion.

This cookbook offers easy, but elegant meals for any event whether a family dinner or an evening soiree. The recipes combine regional foods with the international spices and herbs now so readily available.

HISTORICAL FACTS ON THE CHESAPEAKE BAY REGION

Kitchen – Mount Clare Mansion, Baltimore

"Kissing don't last; cookery do"
George Meredith (1828-1909)

The Bay was formed about 15,000 years ago by glaciers in the Susquehanna Valley. The earliest inhabitants of the Chesapeake area were wanderers that began to settle c 1,000 BC. The creation of the bow and arrow c 500 AD and the cultivation of crops c 800 AD led to permanent villages. The Algonquin were the predominant group with the Susquehannocks just to the north.

The Indians and the early white settlers of the Chesapeake region hunted for geese, venison, turkey; fished in the Chesapeake for eel, rockfish, sturgeon, and bluefish; clammed, oystered, and crabbed. Corn or maize, beans, squash, pumpkins, leeks, watercress, dandelion greens, peas, sweet potatoes, Jerusalem artichokes, and mushrooms were some of the vegetables available. Berries, plums, grapes, melons and other fruits, and nuts such as walnuts, acorns, and chestnuts were gathered. The Powhatan Indians in Virginia grew peanuts, which today is still a viable crop. Parsnips, turnips and carrots were introduced by the English settlers.

Jamestown was the first permanent English settlement in North America, founded in 1607. From here explorers such as John Smith were to explore the Chesapeake Bay taking with them foodstuffs from the settlement. Maryland was founded in 1634 and Delaware in 1638.

The white settlers had to learn to fend for themselves. Disease, malnutrition and lack of agricultural and hunting skills depleted many of the colonies, including Jamestown. Captain John Smith sailed up the Chesapeake in 1608 and "found such an abundance of fish, lying so thick …we attempted to catch them with frying pans."

In 1632 an act of the General Assembly of Virginia ordered free adult men to plant grapevines. Leonard Calvert arrived in St. Mary's, Maryland in 1634, having stopped first in Jamestown to buy cattle, bulls, poultry and hogs. In 1665 King Charles II decreed that European goods could only be imported through England and on English ships bound for the colonies.

Apples and other fruits have been raised in the Chesapeake region for hundreds of years. Apples were first brought to the colonies in the 1600's. They have been eaten raw, baked, cooked in cakes and pies, and numerous other dishes. The earliest apple pie recipe dates from about 1720 in Virginia and was called "poupeton". In 1759 the Virginia colony began exporting Ablemarle pippins (apples) to England.

Later crops included peaches, strawberries, tomatoes, cantaloupes, asparagus, cucumbers, green peas, lima beans, green beans, wheat, rye, barley and potatoes. Tobacco growing depleted much of the nutrients in the soil, and food crops took over. While the Chesapeake and Delaware Canal was being dug, marl, made from decayed seashells was spread by a farmer on his land as a nutrient. Later lime was substituted for this. Crop rotation and fertilizer were also used to nurture the exhausted soil.

During the 1720's and '30's many tobacco plantation owners suffered from a depression, and began raising grains. Like stories from the Bible, wheat was to become a major crop after tobacco in the early days of Maryland. From Genesis 12:10 "And there was a famine in the land; and Abraham went down into Egypt to sojourn there; for the famine was grievous in the land". Until later from Ezekiel 27:17 when times were more prosperous "Judah and the land of Israel, they were thy merchants; they traded in thy market wheat…, and honey, and oil, and balm".

In 1742 Eliza Smith published "The Compleat Housewife, or, Accomplish'd Gentlewoman's Companion of 1727" in Williamsburg. It is thought to be the first cook published in the colonies. Mary Randolph of Virginia published "The Virginia Housewife" in 1824.

In 1752 George Washington inherited Mount Vernon, his brother's plantation. He built a mill that was to become the largest producer of flour in the colonies. Some of the most prominent families had large patents on land, using these estates or plantations to raise a number of crops. European chestnuts were first grown by Thomas

Jefferson at Montpelier, George Washington at Mount Vernon, and Eleuthere Irenee Du Pont in Delaware, Pennsylvania and New Jersey c1800.

Other famous landowners of the region included James Mason of Gunston Hall, the Lee family, James Monroe, and William Fitzhugh of Chatham Manor and "King" Carter of Carter's Grove, near Williamsburg.

Annapolis' staged its own "Tea Party" in 1774 when local patriots forced Anthony Stewart to destroy his vessel, the *Peggy Stewart*, with a cargo of 2,000 pounds of English tea and other goods, by running her aground in Spa Creek and setting fire to her. The Peggy Stewart House is located on Hanover Street in Annapolis. Chestertown had its Tea Party on May 23, 1774 when Chestertown citizens boarded a British ship and dumped its cargo of tea.

Yorktown on the York River was an important port for shipping tobacco and produce. It was here in 1781 that Lord Cornwallis surrendered to the Americans, ending the Revolutionary War.

The Lexington Market in Baltimore was founded in 1792. Today one can shop for any assortment of products. Another favorite place, though not nearly as old is the Cross Street Market on Light Street.

In 1803 Thomas Moore of Maryland received a patent for an ice refrigerator.

The Chesapeake and Delaware Canal connects the Chesapeake Bay and Delaware River providing a means of water transportation for many seafood and agricultural products. The canal was originally proposed in 1654 by Swedish Governor Johann Rising of Delaware. Work was begun in 1804, but later abandoned. The canal was finally finished in 1829. The U.S. government bought the canal in 1919.

The "Farmer's Register" was published in Virginia in 1833 by Edmund Ruffin. It encouraged farmers to rotate their crops, use fertilizers, and not be dependent on the tobacco crop which depleted nutrients in the soil.

Railroads in the mid 19th century were used to carry produce and passengers. Some of the earliest railroad lines were the Baltimore and Ohio Railroad Company that had the first railway passenger cars in

America; the New Castle and Frenchtown Railroad; Wilmington and Susquehanna; the Delaware and Maryland; the Baltimore and Port Deposit; and Wilmington and Baltimore lines. Railroads carried perishable vegetables and fruits, especially peaches, apples, and seafood. Sussex County in Delaware was the main producer of peaches. By 1890 most of the peach crops were destroyed by the "yellows blight".

Major Philip Reybold of Lexington, near New Castle, Delaware was known as the "Peach King" of Delaware and the Eastern Shore of Maryland. In 1845 he owned 117,000 peach trees in two states and shipped the fruit using his own steamers. His farm contained not only peach orchards, but grew grain, cattle, sheep and beans. He served as a contractor for the Chesapeake and Delaware Canal, and used the marl as fertilizer.

Prohibition laws were adopted in Delaware in 1855. In 1862 a federal license was made mandatory for distilling alcohol. Even so moonshiners grew in number. Annapolis was declared a "dry zone" in 1918 by the Secretary of the Navy. No liquor was to be sold within a five mile radius of any naval facility. Saloon owners were fined up to $1000 or jail for one year. For a town that had relied on its many taverns this was devastating news.

In 1861 Isaac Solomon of Baltimore found that he could reduce canning time from six hours to 30 minutes by adding calcium chloride to raise the temperature of boiling water to 240°.

In 1862 the Union army destroyed the Confederate saltworks on the Chesapeake Bay forcing Southerners to find other means of curing pork. In 1863 the Union destroyed the saltworks in Virginia. By 1862 coffee in the South was almost impossible to buy due to the Northern embargo. Peanuts were substituted.

Solomons Island was once known as Somerville Island. It lies one mile from the mouth of the Patuxent River on the north shore. Capt. Isaac Solomon established an oyster business here in 1867, and the area once had a large oyster fleet. Deep water oyster tongs and bugeyes came from here. The J.C. Lore Oyster Processing Plant operated from 1888 to 1978. The causeway is built on a bed of oyster shells.

Crisfield and Baltimore were once considered the oyster capitals of the world. Oystering began in earnest during the Civil War, and was to reach its peak in the 1870's with more than 11 million bushels accounted for. During this time the oystermen of Maryland and Virginia staked out claims on the Bay, which were not settled until 1877 when boundaries were set.

In 1873 Mrs. Benjamin Chew Howard published "Fifty Years in a Maryland Kitchen" in Baltimore. She lived at "Belvidere", part of which was to become the Lexington Market.

Frankfurters were brought to this country from Germany. H.L. Mencken in his book "Happy Days" mentions eating a frankfurter in Baltimore in 1886.

McCormick & Company, Inc. outside Baltimore is the world's largest provider of spices. The company was founded in 1889 Willougby M. McCormick. The first products were sold under the "Bee Brand" and "Silver Medal" brand. Today McCormick produces a number of different spices including Old Bay. Old Wye Island Seasoning and Gary Fairbank's store's seasoning are other popular Chesapeake Bay seasonings, mainly for crab.

Dairy and poultry farms dot the Chesapeake Bay region with the Delmarva Peninsula being the largest producer of chicken in the United States.

In 1994 Maryland banned smoking in restaurants and bars.

Museums to visit that highlight the watermen and their history are the Chesapeake Bay Museum, St. Michael's Maryland; the Mariner's Museum, Newport News, Virginia; the Calvert Marine Museum, Solomons Island, Maryland; Havre de Grace Maritime Museum; and the Watermen's Museum, Rockhall, Maryland.

Displays of waterfowl can be seen at the Ward Museum of Waterfowl Art, Salisbury, Maryland; the Decoy Museum, Havre de Grace, Maryland; and the Chesapeake Bay Maritime Museum, St. Michael's, Maryland.

Henry Louis Mencken, one of Baltimore's greatest writers wrote in 1922 *"To be happy one must be well fed...I lay down the doctrine that it is a sheer impossibility for such a man to live in the United States and not be happy."*

HISTORIC INNS, TAVERNS AND CLUBS

During colonial times establishments that served liquor or meals, or provided lodging had to pay for an ordinary license received from the Circuit Court of Anne Arundel County. The license holder had to provide at least six beds, and provender for ten or more horses. Food and liquor prices were fixed by law. An ordinary was a colonial term for inns and taverns. Indentured servants needed permission from their masters to be served in an inn or tavern. Out-of-town guests could not receive credit for more than 10 shillings.

Gadsby's Tavern in Alexandria, Virginia has operated as a tavern since the late 1700s. General Washington reviewed his troops from the steps of the tavern and Marquis de Lafayette was entertained in 1824.

The Rising Sun Tavern in Fredericksburg, Virginia was built by George Washington's brother, Charles, in 1760.

Williamsburg offers some fine examples of 18th century taverns including Raleigh Tavern and Wetherburn's Tavern. Wetherburn's has the original dairy and a reconstructed kitchen with vegetables grown in the garden. Chownings Tavern is a reconstructed 18th c alehouse that serves Southern specialties such as Brunswick stew and oysters. Christina's Tavern is still serving food after 200+ years.

Surratt House and Tavern, Clinton, Maryland was built in 1852 for John and Mary Surratt. During the Civil War it was a safehouse for the Confederate underground. In 1864 John Wilkes Booth left some of his possessions here. On fleeing from Washington after President Lincoln's assassination, he stopped for them. Mary Surratt was tried as a co-conspirator and on July 7, 1865 became the first woman to be executed by the federal government. The building is now a museum.

Haussner's, a Baltimore landmark restaurant since 1926, sadly closed its doors in 1999. The walls of the restaurant were decorated with world famous paintings, some real, some fake. These and most of the décor were auctioned off by the owners.

The Emerson Hotel (1911-30's) at Baltimore and Calvert Streets, Baltimore, was built by Capt. Isaac Emerson, the inventor of Bromo

Seltzer and builder of the Bromo Tower in Baltimore. The Chesapeake Room was noted for its fine French cuisine.

The Rennert Hotel was built in 1885 at Liberty and Saratoga Streets, Baltimore in 1885. Henry Louis Mencken was a frequent diner. The hotel was the home of the Saturday Night Club.

The Southern Hotel was built in 1918 on Redwood Street, Baltimore, the site of the Fountain Inn. Here in 1781 George Washington and Count de Rochembeau planned the siege of Yorktown. Francis Scott Key stayed here after the bombardment of Ft. McHenry.

The Old Field Inn in Prince Frederick, Maryland was built in 1885 by members of the Briscoe family that once owned Sotterley Plantation in St. Mary's, a most noted plantation.

The Mill House B&B, Northeast, Maryland was built in 1710 as two buildings - one for the miller and the other for the kitchen and servant quarters. The parlor panelling was purchased by Francis duPont for Winterthur.

In 1858 T.M. Harvey's Ladies' and Gentlemen's Oyster Saloon opened in Washington, DC. The restaurant served oysters (the restaurant had its own oyster boats) and terrapin stew, among its offerings.

Just a few miles south of Annapolis on the West River is the charming town of Galesville. Settled in 1649 by Quakers, it was then called West River Landing. It was an "Official Port of Entry" beginning in 1684. In 1699 Francis Wayson settled in Galesville, buying property and building a restaurant and inn. For most of the last three centuries a member of the Wayson family has run an inn, including the present one, the Topside Inn.

The Oxford Inn in Oxford, Maryland and the Inn at Perry Cabin, St. Michael's once served as hangouts for the watermen. Today the Inn at Perry Cabin is owned by the Orient Express and is rated one of the top inns in the United States.

The Columbus Inn is housed in one of the oldest buildings in Wilmington, Delaware, dating from 1798.

The Arsenal on the Green Restaurant in New Castle, Delaware is housed in the Old Arsenal that was built and leased to the government in 1809.

Middleton Tavern, 2 Market Space, Annapolis, was built by Samuel Horatio Middleton in 1745 as a club. Records in 1774 show that the inn had 12 rooms, a separate kitchen and meat house. The Tuesday and Jockey Clubs met here. Later it was a tavern and store selling Madeira, rum, molasses, sugar, beer and even lemons. The present tavern has been run by Joseph Hardesty since 1968. James Gross has been an employee since 1948.

Reynolds Tavern, Church Circle, Annapolis was opened in 1747 by William Reynolds who leased the land from St. Anne's Parish. The building has been a hattery, bank, restaurant and library. The building is owned by the National Trust for Historic Preservation, but has a lease with the Historic Annapolis Foundation until 2076 for $1 per annum.

The Maryland Inn, Annapolis, Maryland dates from 1772 and was built as a tavern and inn by Thomas Hyde. Records show that the King of France Tavern was operated by Sarah Ball in 1784.

During the 18th c the Shiplap House, 18 Pinkney Street, Annapolis was run as an inn by Edward Smith. In 1787 it was rented to John Humphrey as the tavern "at the Sign of the Harp and Crown".

The first coffee house in Annapolis was the Maryland Coffee House opened in 1767 by Cornelius Howard at 200 Main Street.

Armadillo's Restaurant, Annapolis, was once a jailhouse. The lovely brick building is over 200 years old.

O'Brien's, 113 Main Street, Annapolis was built in 1774. It later became the Rose and Crown, then Fran O'Brien's, and a bowling alley. During the 1980's unfortunately much of the building was destroyed by fire, but has been rebuilt.

Rumney's Tavern, once located at London Town, and owned by Edward and Elinor Rumney, served victuals from the 1690s until 1720, when it was taken over by Stephen West.

The City Dock, Annapolis has been in use since 1650 as a dock. The Ship Carpenter's lot was to the left of City Dock. Skipjacks, bugeyes, and other vessels used in the seafood industry, tied up here.

The Market Place, Annapolis is the fifth edifice built on the site. The present one was built in 1858. A site was selected as early as 1684, but no building existed. In 1717 the first Market House opened on State Circle. In 1784 filled land on the dock was deeded by eight Annapolis residents for use as a market, which is still maintained. Records show the market master was also the town lamplighter. The lamp finials were in the shape of tobacco leaves.

Sam Lewnes moved to Annapolis in 1912 and in 1920 opened Sam's Corner, a luncheonette, at Fourth Street and Severn Avenue in Eastport. The business was turned over to his sons, Louis and George, in 1947 and renamed Lewnes' Bar and Grill. In 1955 George Lewnes opened a Greek restaurant, The Bridgeview, at Sixth Street and Severn Avenue. In the 1960s they were joined by their sons Charlie and Spiro. Lou Lewnes changed the luncheonette's name to Lou's Restaurant. With the closing of the Trumpy Boat Yard in 1973 Lou's lost most of its customers and closed. Charlie Lewnes bought the property in 1988, once again as Sam's Corner. In 1994 this became Lewnes' Steak House.

The South River Club, near London Town, Maryland was built c1740 and is thought to be the first social club in continuous use. The men's social club meets four times a year for dinner.

Each city had its own gentlemen's clubs that met on a regular basis. Punch, Sherry, Port, Rum, or Madeira would be served, followed by a meal, song, or "discussion".

The idea of fox hunt clubs was brought over from England, along with hounds. The second oldest hunt is the Elkridge Hounds at Long Quarter Farm in the Dulaney Valley, Maryland, which was established in 1872. I often remember my uncles riding to the hunt on Thanksgiving morning, very early, and returning smartly fed and liquored up, long before dinner was even to be served! New Year's morning they also gathered for the hunt.

Other men's societies were to spring up such as the Gourmet Society (to which my grandparents belonged and often brought along my parents); the Agricultural Society; the Society of Colonial Wars in

13

Maryland, Virginia and Delaware; and the Maryland Jockey Club, all of which served elaborate and many course meals.

Ladies were not left out, but were to join the Colonial Dames, Junior League, or other civic organizations. At their functions, tea or luncheons were elaborately laid out and served.

CHESAPEAKE REGION WINERIES

Delaware, Maryland and Virginia have grown grapes since colonial times. But only recently have they received some recognition.

Maryland
Gov. Calvert of Maryland brought vines from France in 1662 and planted them on 200 acres. His best grape was called the "Alexander".

In 1942 Philip Wagner opened Boordy Vineyards in Maryland. He was an editorial columnist with the Baltimore Sun and went on to write the book "American Wines and How to Make Them" and "Grapes into Wine".

Today Maryland produces about 450 tons of grapes, about 300,000 bottles of wine. Wineries include Fiore Winery, Pykesville; Elk Run Vineyard and Winery, Mount Airy; Boordy Vineyard, Hydes; Basignani Winery, Sparks; and Woodhall Wine Cellars, Parkton.

Virginia
Wines were believed to have been produced as early as 1609. In 1773 Thomas Jefferson raised Italian grapes and designed his own wine cooler, which is on display at Monticello.

Virginia Wineries near the Chesapeake include Windy River Winery, Beaverdam; The Williamsburg Winery, Williamsburg; and Ingleside Plantation Vineyards, Oak Grove.

Delaware
One of the grapes grown in the United States is known as the Delaware grape. This labrusca or table wine has low acidity and is somewhat bitter. However, the wine is not grown in Delaware, but Ohio!

The Delaware wineries include Nassau Valley Vineyards, Nassau and Felton Crest, Felton.

APPETIZERS

Chesapeake Bay Oysters – Tilghman Island, Maryland

Cocktail Party

Smoked Salmon/Capers/Onions/Toast
Crudites and Dips
Crab Dip
Pate
Baked Brie
French Bread
Brownies

CRAB DIP WITH ALMONDS

8 ounces cream cheese
1 tablespoon milk
2 tsp. Worcestershire sauce

2 tablespoons minced onion
1 pound fresh crab meat
¼ cup toasted almonds

- ◆ Soften the cream cheese with milk in a bowl, and then add the Worcestershire sauce, onions and crab meat, being careful not to break up the crab meat.
- ◆ Place in a crab shaped or oval baking dish.
- ◆ Sprinkle with the toasted almonds.
- ◆ Bake in 350° oven for 20 minutes, until just slightly browned on top. Serve with crackers.

CRAB DIP WITH ARTICHOKE HEARTS

1½ cups sour cream
1 tablespoon lemon juice
¼ teaspoon Tabasco Sauce
1 pound crab meat

1 large can artichoke hearts
½ cup fresh Parmesan cheese
1 teaspoon fresh dill

- ◆ Finely grate the parmesan cheese.
- ◆ Combine all ingredients in a bowl until well blended.
- ◆ Cover and refrigerate overnight. Serve with crackers.

CHEESY CRAB DIP

1 pound fresh crab meat
8 ounces cream cheese
½ cup sour cream
1 tablespoon lemon juice

1 tsp. Worcestershire sauce
½ tsp. dry mustard
¼ cup grated cheddar cheese
1 clove garlic, crushed

- Preheat oven to 325°.
- Combine all ingredients except crab meat. Fold in crab meat.
- Pour into a casserole dish and bake for 20 minutes or until browned on top.
- Serve with crackers.

LEEK CRAB DIP

1½ cups sour cream
1 tablespoon lemon juice
¼ teaspoon Tabasco sauce
1 package leek soup mix

1 pound fresh crab meat
14 ounce can artichoke hearts
½ cup parmesan cheese
1 tablespoon fresh dill

- Drain the liquid from the artichoke hearts
- In a medium sized bowl combine all the ingredients.
- Refrigerate overnight.
- Serve at room temperature with rye rounds or sliced French bread.
- Serving this in a cut out round loaf of bread makes for an easy serving dish and convenient bread dipper.

CURRIED CRAB DIP

1 pound fresh crab meat
8 ounces cream cheese
½ cup sour cream

1 tablespoon lemon juice
1 teaspoon curry powder

- Preheat oven to 325°.
- Combine all the ingredients except crab meat. Fold in the crab meat.
- Pour into a casserole dish and bake for 20 minutes or until browned on top. Serve with crackers.

MINIATURE CRAB CAKES

16 crab cakes

1 pound crab meat
2 tablespoons bread crumbs
1 egg
1 teaspoon Worcestershire

1 teaspoon Dijon mustard
2 tablespoons mayonnaise
Dash of Old Bay Seasoning
Butter

- ◆ With a fork carefully combine the ingredients in a bowl. Shape into small cakes.
- ◆ Saute in butter until brown on each side.
- ◆ Serve on rounds cut out with a cookie cutter or small rimmed glass.
- ◆ Garnish with tartar sauce, thin lemon slices or a sprig of parsley.

CRAB STUFFED MUSHROOMS

½ pound fresh crab meat
1 container boursin cheese
1 pound mushrooms

1 tablespoon fresh parsley
2 tablespoons sherry

- ◆ Preheat oven to 350°
- ◆ Remove stems from the mushrooms. Chop the stems finely and put in a bowl. Add cheese, parsley, sherry and crab meat.
- ◆ Place the caps on a cookie sheet. Fill the mushroom caps with the crab mixture.
- ◆ Bake for 15 minutes or until just browned.

SNOW PEAS WITH CRAB

1 pound snow peas

½ pound crab salad

- ◆ Slit snow peas along one side and insert a small amount of crab salad.
- ◆ Serve on a crab shaped dish or white serving plate garnished with paprika or parsley.

SNOW PEAS WITH BLUE CHEESE

1 pound snow peas
½ pound blue cheese, crumbled

3 ounces cream cheese

- ♦ Slit snow peas along one side.
- ♦ Combine the cheeses. Carefully stuff the cheeses in snow pea slit.

OYSTER CEVICHE

Serves 4-6

24 oysters with liquor
¼ cup red pepper, chopped
¼ cup green pepper, chopped
Juice of 1 lime
Lime slices

¼ cup red onion
2 tablespoons parsley
2 tomatoes, diced
½ cup seafood sauce
1 cup diced avocado

- ♦ Drain the oysters and pour the liquor in a saucepan. Bring to a boil, reduce heat and add the oysters. Poach for 2 minutes.
- ♦ Drain the liquor. Place the oysters in a bowl. Squeeze the lime over the oysters.
- ♦ Add the peppers, onion, parsley, tomatoes and avocado.
- ♦ Stir in the chili sauce.
- ♦ Serve in the cleaned oyster shells or small separate dishes garnished with the lime slices.

OYSTER AND BACON APPETIZERS

1 pint oysters
½ pound bacon

Toothpicks

- ♦ Cup the bacon strips into thirds.
- ♦ Wrap each strip around an oyster. Hold with a toothpick.
- ♦ Place in an oven proof baking dish. Grill under broiler until bacon is crisp or heat until bacon is crisp in 400° oven.
- ♦ (Mussels, smoked oysters, or scallops can be substituted for the oysters).

LILI'S TORTILLA ROLL-UPS

6 large tortillas
8 ounces cream cheese
½ cup chopped black olives

1 cup grated cheddar cheese
½ pound crab meat

- Mix cheeses, olives and crab in a bowl.
- Spread on tortillas. Roll up tortillas. Cut into ½ inch pieces.
- Serve with salsa or plain.
- Finely chopped shrimp can be substituted for the crab.

CLAM DIP

1 pint clams
8 ounces cream cheese

½ cup sour cream
¼ cup horseradish

- Combine all the ingredients in a bowl.
- This can be served cold with crackers, or baked in an oven at 350° for 20 minutes or until just browned.

CLAMS CASINO

2 dozen small clams
¼ cup fresh parsley, chopped
¼ cup green peppers
¼ cup chopped celery

¼ cup onion, chopped
¼ teaspoon cayenne
4 strips bacon

- Preheat oven to 300°. Place the clams in the oven until the shell opens.
- In a skillet cook the bacon and reserve the fat. Add the vegetables and cook until tender. Add the cayenne.
- Remove one shell from each clam and top the clam with the vegetable mixture. Broil until bubbling.

SMOKED BLUEFISH

Bluefish filets

- Heat up smoker and place the bluefish on the grill, with the skin facing towards the grill.
- Smoke two hours.
- Chill fish before serving

Mustard Sauce

½ cup Dijon mustard
¼ teaspoon coarse salt
¼ cup honey

Juice of ½ lemon
2 tablespoons olive oil
Cracked black pepper to taste

- In a bowl combine all the ingredients.
- Apply mustard sauce liberally to fish while smoking.
- Reserve some sauce to serve with appetizer.

SMOKED BLUEFISH PATE

1 pound smoked bluefish
2 scallions
8 ounces cream cheese

Juice of 1 lemon
Fresh dill

- Remove the skin from the fish.
- Place the fish in a food processor and pulse for a short time until broken up. Add scallion, lemon juice and cream cheese.
- Remove from processor and chill overnight. Place in a serving dish and garnish with fresh chopped dill.
- Serve with crackers.

SMOKED FISH

- Any kind of fish, mussels, oysters, or clams can be smoked.
- There are a number of good smokers available.
- Serve the fish with a sauce and bread, and you have an easy appetizer.

CRUDITES AND DIPS

During the year the Chesapeake has a wide variety of fresh vegetables that can be used as appetizers. Different colored peppers add color to any tray. Fresh herbs (dry can be substituted) add wonderful flavors to the dip.

HERB DIP

1 cup sour cream
2 large crushed garlic cloves

1 tsp. Worcestershire sauce
1 tablespoon mixed herbs

♦ Combine all ingredients in a small bowl. Cover and refrigerate overnight.

CURRY DIP

1 cup sour cream
2 large garlic cloves
2 teaspoons curry

½ teaspoon cumin
½ teaspoon ginger

♦ Combine all ingredients in a small bowl. Cover and refrigerate overnight.

LEEK DIP

1 cup sour cream

½ package leek soup mix

♦ Combine all ingredients in a small bowl. Cover and refrigerate overnight.

CHIVE DIP

½ cup mayonnaise
½ cup sour cream
¼ cup fresh chopped parsley
2 tablespoon chopped chives

1 Tbls. white wine vinegar
1 tablespoon lemon juice
1 clove garlic, mashed

- Combine all ingredients in a small bowl. Cover and refrigerate overnight.

SPICY DIP

8 ounces cream cheese
4 tablespoons sour cream
Salt and pepper to taste
½ teaspoon Tabasco sauce

½ teaspoon paprika
1 Tbls. Worcestershire sauce
¼ cup parsley, chopped

- Combine all ingredients in a bowl and serve with a variety of fresh vegetables.

CHIPPED BEEF DIP

8 ounces chipped beef
8 ounces cream cheese
1 cup sour cream

2 scallions, chopped
¼ cup pecans

- Combine chipped beef, sour cream and onion in a bowl.
- Put in a baking dish that can be used as a serving dish.
- Top with pecans. Bake at 350° for 20 minutes.
- Serve with crackers or sliced French bread.

STUFFED DATES

1 container dates   Sugar
Pecans or almonds

- ◆ Cut slit in dates and insert a nut in each.
- ◆ Sprinkle with a small amount of sugar.
- ◆ Serve on a silver platter.

GINGER AND PECAN STUFFED DATES

1 container dates   Crystallized ginger
Pecans

- ◆ Cut slit in dates and insert a nut and piece of ginger in each.
- ◆ Serve on a silver platter.

GINGER STUFFED DATES

1 container dates   1 cup crystallized ginger
8 ounces cream cheese

- ◆ Mix together cream cheese and ginger.
- ◆ Cut slit in dates. Stuff with cream cheese mixture.

Summer Garden Party

Stuffed Mushrooms
Lili's Chicken Liver Pate with French Bread
Cucumber Sandwiches
Watercress Sandwiches
Spinach Squares

LILI'S CHICKEN LIVER PATE

1 pound chicken liver
1 stick butter
¼ cup bourbon
Dash of nutmeg and allspice
1 small onion, chopped

½ teaspoon salt
¼ teaspoon ground cloves

- Boil the chicken livers until light pink and tender.
- Put all the ingredients in a food processor until well blended.
- Line a round mold or bread pan with wax paper. Pour in the pate mixture.
- Chill until firm. Unmold and serve with sliced French bread.

PATE

1 pound chicken livers
¼ cup butter
½ pound mushrooms, sliced
½ cup scallions, sliced
1 teaspoon salt
½ cup white wine

1 large clove garlic, crushed
½ teaspoon fresh rosemary
½ teaspoon fresh dill
½ teaspoon dry mustard
½ cup butter, softened

- Melt ¼ cup butter in skillet. Add chicken livers, mushrooms and onions. Saute for 5 minutes.
- Add wine, garlic, mustard, rosemary and dill. Cover and simmer for 10 minutes. Then cook until almost all the liquid is absorbed.
- In food processor blend chicken liver mixture and ½ cup butter until smooth.
- Put in bowl and refrigerate. Serve with toasted French bread or crackers.

CHICKEN LIVER AND BACON APPETIZERS

1 pound chicken livers   Toothpicks
½ pound bacon

- ◆ Cut the bacon strips into three pieces.
- ◆ Wrap the bacon around the chicken livers and hold with toothpicks.
- ◆ Place in a baking dish.
- ◆ Grill under broiler until bacon is crisp.

DATE AND BACON APPETIZERS

1 pound pitted dates   Toothpicks
½ pound bacon

- ◆ Cut the bacon strips into three pieces.
- ◆ Wrap the bacon around the dates and hold with toothpicks.
- ◆ Place in a baking dish and grill under broiler until bacon is crisp.

WATER CHESTNUT APPETIZERS

2 cans whole water chestnuts   Toothpicks
½ pound bacon

- ◆ Cut the bacon strips into three pieces.
- ◆ Wrap the bacon around the water chestnuts and hold with toothpicks.
- ◆ Place in baking dish and grill under broiler until bacon is crisp.

WATERMELON PICKLE AND BACON

1 large jar watermelon pickle   Toothpicks
½ pound bacon

- Cut the bacon strips into three pieces.
- Wrap the bacon around each pickle slice and hold with a toothpick. Pour a small amount of the pickle juice over the pickles.
- Place on a baking sheet and grill under broiler until the bacon is crisp.

BACON WRAPPED STICKS

1 package thin bread sticks   ½ pound bacon

- Brown the bacon in a skillet until just slightly browned and not crisp.
- Wrap each bread stick with a slice of bacon.
- Place under the broiler until just browned.

BAKED BRIE

1 small round brie   ½ cup pecans
¼ cup brown sugar   2 tablespoons melted butter
1 package crescent rolls

- Take the brie out of the refrigerator at least one hour before preparing to allow to soften.
- Roll out the crescent rolls (don't separate) so that it is approximately the size of a pie.
- Place the brie on the rolled out dough and sprinkle with brown sugar and pecans. Fold the edges of the pastry around the cheese. Brush with melted butter.
- Bake in 425° oven for 10 minutes, or crust is just brown. Let stand for 10 minutes.
- Place on serving dish and serve with crackers or French bread.
- Apples and grapes can be used as garnish.

CHEESE BALL

2 8 oz packages cream cheese
½ pound blue cheese
¼ cup onion, grated

1 tsp. Worcestershire sauce
Salt and pepper, to taste
½ cup walnuts, pecans or parsley, chopped

- Take the cream cheese out of the refrigerator at least one hour ahead of preparation to soften.
- Place the cream cheese in a bowl and add salt and pepper. Stir in onion and Worcestershire sauce. Blend in the blue cheese that has been crumbled.
- Mold into a ball. Roll in nuts or parsley. Refrigerate.
- Serve with crackers or assorted breads.

HAM AND CHEESE CALZONE

3½ cups flour
1 package dry yeast
1 cup lukewarm water

1 teaspoon olive oil
½ teaspoon salt

- Preheat oven to 500°.
- Soften yeast in the water.
- In a food processor put the flour. Slowly add the yeast and olive oil until a ball is formed.
- In an oiled bowl let the dough rise for one hour or until doubled.
- On an oiled cookie sheet flatten the dough until it almost covers pan and let rise ½ hour.

Filling

1 cup ham, chopped
1 cup grated cheddar cheese

1 tablespoon rosemary
1 egg beaten

- Combine the ham, cheese and rosemary in a bowl.
- Spread the ham mixture over the dough. Roll dough up lengthwise. Brush with beaten egg.
- Bake 20 minutes or until browned. Serve hot or cold.

KAY'S FAKE BOURSIN

1 stick butter
1 clove garlic, crushed
1 teaspoon parsley

1 teaspoon dill
8 ounces cream cheese

- ◆ Combine all ingredients in a bowl.
- ◆ Shape into a mold. Refrigerate overnight.
- ◆ Serve with crackers or French bread.

GA'S CHEESE ROLL

½ pound cheddar cheese
½ stick butter
½ teaspoon salt

1¼ cup flour
1 cup Rice Krispies

- ◆ Preheat oven to 325°.
- ◆ Combine all ingredients in a bowl. Form into a log.
- ◆ Slice and place on a cookie sheet. Bake for 10 minutes.

CHEESE PUFFS

1¾ cups Bisquick
1 pound fresh sausage

1 cup sharp cheddar cheese

- ◆ Place all ingredients in a food processor and mix thoroughly.
- ◆ Form into golf-size balls.
- ◆ Place on baking sheet and bake 350° for 20 minutes.

BLUE CHEESE SPREAD

1 pound blue cheese
¼ cup apple cider

¼ cup fresh lemon juice
4 tart green apples

♦ With a fork crumble the blue cheese in a bowl and add the cider.
♦ Core the apples and cut into thin slices. Put the apples into a large bowl filled with water and the lemon juice.
♦ When ready to serve, pat the apple slices dry with paper towels.
♦ Spread the cheese mixture on the apples. Serve immediately.

CHEESY CHUTNEY DIP

2 8 oz. packages cream cheese
¼ cup chutney
½ cup toasted almonds

4 teaspoons curry
½ teaspoon dry mustard

♦ Combine all ingredients together in a bowl and refrigerate.
♦ Serve with crackers.

RUTHIE'S CHILI DIP

1 can chili without beans
1 small onion, chopped

8 ounces cream cheese
½ lb. Monterey Jack cheese

♦ Heat oven to 350°.
♦ Spread the cream cheese on the bottom of a glass pie plate.
♦ Spread the chopped onion over cream cheese.
♦ Then put on a layer of grated Monterey Jack cheese.
♦ Spread the chili on top of this.
♦ Bake 20 minutes, or until bubbling. Serve with tortilla or corn chips
♦ For a party this recipe is double and served in a 13" x 9" inch baking dish.

BLINI

1 large jar red or black caviar
1 small onion, finely chopped

1 recipe "Flyaway Pancakes"
8 ounce container sour cream

- ◆ Make quarter-size pancakes from the "Flyaway Pancake" recipe. Place on a serving dish.
- ◆ Cover each pancake with a dollop of sour cream. Spoon caviar on top.
- ◆ At New Year's we like to use both red and black caviar.

KAY'S CAVIAR PIE

When we were very young and lived in New Castle, Delaware, my parents had a party. The next morning we three children sneaked downstairs and raided the refrigerator. Thinking we were eating blueberries and ice cream we were in for a real surprise to find out it was caviar and sour cream.

4 hard boiled eggs
¼ cup butter, melted
1 cup sour cream

1 tablespoon onion, minced
1 jar black or red caviar

- ◆ In a pie plate mash the eggs with melted butter and shape into a crust. Put in the refrigerator until firm.
- ◆ Combine the sour cream with onion and spread over the egg mixture.
- ◆ Spread the caviar on top.
- ◆ Serve with crackers, melba toast, or French bread.

RUSSIAN EGGS

1 dozen eggs
1 tablespoon Dijon mustard
¼ cup or less mayonnaise

Salt and pepper
1 jar red or black caviar

- ◆ Hard boil the eggs and let cool. Slice in half.
- ◆ On top of the eggs spoon some caviar, either black or red.
- ◆ Serve on a silver tray covered with a doily, as silver tarnishes from eggs.

Hunt Cup Repast

Champagne
Mint Juleps
Deviled Eggs
Fried Chicken
Mixed Spring Greens Salad
Brownies

DEVILED EGGS

1 dozen eggs
1 tablespoon Dijon mustard
¼ cup or less mayonnaise

Salt and pepper
¼ cup parsley, chopped

- ♦ Hard boil the eggs and let cool.
- ♦ Slice the eggs in half.
- ♦ Remove the yolks and place in a bowl. Add the mustard, salt and pepper. Put the eggs on a platter. Spoon the yolk mixture over eggs. Garnish with parsley.
- ♦ 1 teaspoon curry powder can be added for a spicier egg and flavor.

GA'S STUFF O' NONSENSE

1 box Rice Chex
1 box Cheerios
1 box Kix
1 box Shredded Wheat
1 tablespoon butter, melted
1 tablespoon garlic powder

1 teaspoon chili powder
1 tablespoon Tabasco
1 large can mixed nuts
1 large bag pretzel sticks
1 Tbls. Worcestershire sauce

- ♦ Combine all ingredients in a large baking dish. (A roasting pan works best).
- ♦ Bake in 200° oven for 1¼ hours. Keep an eye on this, so it doesn't burn.

ROASTED PECANS

1 pound pecans
4 tablespoons butter

Salt

♦ Preheat oven to 350°.
♦ Melt butter in baking dish. Add pecans and toss in butter.
♦ Bake in oven for 15 minutes. Salt for taste.

SPICY PECANS

1 pound pecans
1 teaspoon cumin
½ cup melted butter

½ teaspoon cayenne
1 teaspoon coarse salt
¼ cup sugar

♦ Spread pecans in a baking dish. Sprinkle in cumin and cayenne and then pour the butter over the nuts. Toss to coat all the pecans. Sprinkle the salt and sugar on top.
♦ Bake 30 minutes at 300°. Be careful not to burn the nuts.

PUMPKIN SPREAD

This unusual spread is perfect for a fall party.

16 ounces cream cheese
2 cups pumpkin
¾ cup sugar

1 teaspoon vanilla
1 teaspoon cinnamon
½ teaspoon ginger
½ teaspoon nutmeg

♦ Combine all the ingredients. Serve with gingersnaps.

PESTO TORTELLINI

2 packages frozen tortellini (can be chicken, beef or cheese)

½ cup pesto sauce

♦ Cook the tortellini according to directions on the package.
♦ In a bowl toss together the tortellini and pesto.
♦ Serve with toothpicks.

EMPANADAS

1 pound ground lamb or beef
1 small onion, chopped
¼ cup pine nuts
2 hard boiled eggs, chopped

8 green olives, chopped
½ teaspoon oregano
Tabasco to taste

♦ In a pan saute the meat and onions. Cool. Add the rest of the ingredients.

Pastry

3 ½ cups flour
½ cup butter

½ cup water
¼ teaspoon salt

♦ Heat oven to 400°
♦ In a food processor place the flour and butter. Slowly add the water until a ball is formed
♦ On a floured board roll out the dough. Use a glass or round cutter to cut out round shapes.
♦ On each round place a teaspoon of the meat mixture. Fold over and seal with just a small amount of water.
♦ Place the empanadas on a cookie sheet. Bake 15 minutes or until browned.

PEANUT BUTTER FINGERS

An old family friend always served these delicious "fingers".

6 slices thin bread
½ cup peanut butter

½ cup butter
Bread crumbs

♦ Remove the crusts from the bread and cut in ½ inch "fingers".
♦ Put on a cookie sheet. Place in 250° oven until toasted.
♦ In a double boiler melt the butter and peanut butter.
♦ Dip the "fingers" into the mixture.
♦ Cool on wax paper. Dip in bread crumbs. Refrigerate in a tightly sealed container.

LILI'S EGGPLANT CAPONATA

4 tablespoons olive oil
1 large eggplant, cut into cubes,
peel left on
1 medium onion, minced
1/3 cup celery
1 cup tomato puree
½ can black olives

1 can anchovies
2 tablespoons capers
2 tablespoons vinegar
1 tablespoon sugar
½ teaspoon salt
¼ teaspoon pepper
Parsley, minced

- ♦ Heat the oil in a large frying pan. Add the eggplant and saute 10 minutes (the eggplant may soak up the olive oil and more oil may need to be added).
- ♦ Add the onion and celery and fry until golden. Add remaining ingredients, except parsley.
- ♦ Cover and simmer for 1½ hours. Stir in parsley and cool.
- ♦ This can be served as a side dish or as an hors d'oeuvre with crackers.

SPINACH SQUARES

1½ pounds fresh spinach
1 bunch scallions, chopped
1 large onion, chopped
1 tablespoon olive oil
¼ cup fresh parsley

¼ cup fresh dill
1 pound feta cheese
6 eggs
1 pound phyllo pastry
2 sticks butter, melted

- ♦ Preheat oven to 350°.
- ♦ Wash spinach and remove stems. Dry on paper towels.
- ♦ Brown the onions and scallion in oil until tender.
- ♦ In a bowl combine the spinach, parsley, dill, scallions, onions, cheese and eggs, mixing well.
- ♦ Grease a 9 x 13 inch baking dish and line with ½ of the phyllo, brushing with butter.
- ♦ Spread the spinach mixture over the phyllo and cover with the rest of the phyllo.
- ♦ Bake in oven for one hour.
- ♦ Cut into squares and serve hot or cold.
- ♦ This is also very good using cheddar or mozzarella cheese instead of the feta. To add a bite to it, use Monterey Jack cheese with green peppers.

GUACAMOLE

2 large ripe avocados
Juice of one lemon
¼ cup red onion

3 large cloves garlic, crushed
1 teaspoon chili powder

- Mash the avocado with a fork. Add other ingredients. Place in a bowl.
- Serve immediately with tortilla or corn chips.

BRUSCHETTA

There are many ways to make bruschetta, but this one is best served during the summer when the tomatoes are ripe.

2 large tomatoes
2 cloves garlic
2 Tbls. fresh basil, chopped

Salt and pepper to taste
¼ cup olive oil
1 French bread baguette

- Finely chop the tomatoes, garlic and basil in a bowl. Add salt, pepper and olive oil.
- Cut the baguette into ½ inch slices and toast under broiler.
- Spread the tomato mixture on the bread
- Serve immediately.
- This can also be put back under the broiler until bubbly.
- Fresh grated parmesan cheese can be sprinkled on top.

MUSHROOMS STUFFED WITH PATE

1 pound mushrooms
3 ounce package cream cheese

1 can liver pate
2 tablespoons sherry

- Preheat oven to 350°.
- Cut the stems off the mushrooms.
- Combine the pate, cream cheese and sherry.
- Place the mushrooms on a cookie sheet. Stuff the mushrooms with the pate mixture.
- Bake in oven for 15 minutes.

MUSHROOMS WITH SAUSAGE

Mushrooms are not grown in the Chesapeake Bay region, but come from nearby Pennsylvania.

1 pound mushrooms
½ pound sausage

¼ cup Italian bread crumbs

- ♦ Preheat oven to 350°.
- ♦ Cook the sausage in a skillet.
- ♦ Take the stems off the mushrooms and chop finely.
- ♦ Add the stems and bread crumbs to the sausage.
- ♦ Stuff mushrooms with the mixture and place in a baking dish.
- ♦ Bake in oven 15 minutes.

MUSHROOMS WITH CHEESE

1 pound mushrooms
2 tablespoons butter
3 ounces cream cheese
3 ounces blue cheese

2 tablespoons scallion, chopped
¼ teaspoon fine herbes
Paprika

- ♦ Clean the mushrooms and remove the stems. Finely chop the stems in a bowl.
- ♦ In a skillet saute the mushrooms. Remove from the heat and add the cheeses, scallion and fine herbes.
- ♦ Stuff the mushroom caps with the mixture.
- ♦ Place under broiler until bubbling.

MUSHROOM TOAST

1 pound mushrooms, chopped
8 ounces cream cheese

¼ cup scallions, chopped
Thin sliced white bread loaf

- ♦ Remove the crusts from the bread. Cut the bread diagonally across. Put on a cookie sheet and toast on each side.
- ♦ Combine the mushrooms, cream cheese and scallions. Spread on toast.
- ♦ Put under broiler until bubbling.

FRIED WONTON

1 pound shrimp, chicken or sausage,
2 tablespoons sesame oil
1 can sliced water chestnuts
2 green onions

2 tablespoons dry Sherry
2 cloves garlic, crushed
2 tablespoons soy sauce
1 package wonton wrappers
Vegetable oil

- In a food processor blend together the shrimp (chicken or sausage), water chestnuts, onions, sherry and garlic.
- In a wok heat the sesame oil. Stir in the shrimp or meat mixture for 30 seconds.
- Spoon one teaspoon of the meat mixture onto the middle of each wonton wrapper. Seal edges with water.
- Fry in vegetable oil in the wok until crisp. Do not let the oil get too hot as the wonton will burn quickly.

GEORGE'S SALSA

6 large tomatoes
1 bunch green onions
1 green pepper
1 tablespoon fresh cilantro

1 tablespoon vinegar
2 cloves garlic
4 jalapeno peppers
Salt and pepper to taste

- Finely chop the tomatoes and place in a large mixing bowl.
- Dice the pepper and finely chop the green onions. Remove the seeds from the jalapenos and mince. Add to the tomatoes.
- Stir in the rest of the ingredients. Serve with tortilla chips

MEATBALLS IN SALSA

2 pounds ground beef
½ cup onion, chopped
½ cup bread crumbs

Salt and pepper
Salsa (see recipe above)

- In a bowl combine the beef, onion, bread crumbs, salt and pepper to taste. Shape the meat into golf-size balls.
- Brown the meatballs in a skillet.
- Heat the salsa in a saucepan. Put meatballs and salsa in a chaffing dish. Serve warm with toothpicks.

"I've made it a rule never to drink by daylight and never to refuse a drink after dark."
Henry Louis Mencken (1880-1956)

Wine Cooler - Mount Clare Mansion

SPECIAL DRINKS

The earliest drinks served in the clubs and at home were punches, especially rum, port, Spanish wine, sherry and Madeira.

In 1789 bourbon whiskey was first distilled by Elijah Craig, a Baptist minister in Kentucky County, Virginia, later to become Bourbon County, Kentucky.

RASPBERRY SHRUB

1 quart raspberry juice   1 pint dark rum
½ pound sugar

- ◆ Combine the ingredients. Store in a bottle. Refrigerate.
- ◆ ½ pint rum and ½ pint brandy can be substituted for the rum.
- ◆ Serve in tall glasses filled with crushed ice.

PLANTER'S PUNCH

Serves 8

1 bottle dark rum   1 quart pineapple juice
1 quart orange juice   Lemon or lime slices

- ◆ In a large pitcher combine the rum and juices.
- ◆ Serve in glasses over ice with a lemon or lime slice.

New Year's Eve Party

Caviar Eggs
Blini
Hot Crab Meat Dip
Baked Brie and Assorted Breads
Smithfield Ham with Biscuits
Smoked Salmon
Fish House Punch

FISH HOUSE PUNCH

This is our favorite punch to serve for a Christmas or garden party. Please be careful as it is very strong and a cup or two can make a guest a little tipsy.

Fish House Punch was concocted at the Fish House Club in Philadelphia c1732. This rum punch was to become a favorite for parties and clubs.

1 round ice mold	1 bottle dark rum
1 cup sugar	1 bottle light rum
8 cups tea	1 bottle Cognac
3 cups lemon juice	1 cup peach brandy

- Combine all ingredients in a large punch bowl.
- Just before serving place the ice mold in a punch bowl. Serve the punch in punch cups.

BLOODY MARY

1 bottle V-8 juice	¼ cup horseradish
2 cups vodka	Salt and pepper to taste
¼ cup lemon juice	Celery
1 Tbls. Worcestershire sauce	

- Combine all the ingredients except the celery in a pitcher.
- Put ice cubes in tall glasses. Pour the Bloody Mary mix over ice. Serve with a stalk of celery.

RON'S CHRISTMAS EGGNOG

7 eggs
¾ cup sugar
1 pint heavy cream
2 cups milk

2 cups bourbon
¼ cup dark rum
Freshly grated nutmeg

- Separate the eggs. Beat the yolks in a bowl. Add ½ cup sugar to the yolks.
- In another bowl beat the egg whites until stiff and add ¼ cup sugar.
- Fold the egg whites into the egg yolk mixture. Fold in the cream and milk.
- Slowly add the bourbon and rum, and stir thoroughly.
- Serve cold in a punch bowl with grated nutmeg.

RUM CIDER

1 gallon cider
1 bottle dark rum

2 sticks cinnamon

- In a large pot heat the cider and cinnamon.
- Pour into a punch bowl and add the rum. Serve in punch cups.

MULLED CIDER

1 gallon cider
12 whole cloves

4 cinnamon sticks
1 lemon, thinly sliced

- Pour the cider into a large pot. Add cinnamon and cloves.
- Boil and then let simmer 5 minutes.
- Pour into a heatproof punchbowl with lemon slices floating on top. Serve in punch cups.

CIDER PUNCH

Makes about 30 cups

1 bottle rum
1 gallon apple cider

1 large bottle ginger ale
2 apples, cored and sliced

- ◆ Combine rum and cider in a punch bowl and refrigerate.
- ◆ When ready to serve add ginger ale. Top with apple slices.

PEACH DAIQUIRIS

Serves 4

2 pounds peaches, peeled and
cut up

1 cup dark rum
Ice

- ◆ Place the peaches and rum in a food processor. Blend until smooth.
- ◆ Served in glasses over crushed ice.

BANANA DAIQUIRIS

Not long after I moved to Cleveland in the mid 1970's my three former brothers-in-law came to help me cook dinner, since their mother was in the hospital. Doug, the youngest, suggested we make banana daiquiris. They were so good that I forgot to put in the second package of cream cheese into the mincemeat cheesecake. I kept wondering why it was so runny, until the next morning I found the other package in the refrigerator. So be forewarned!

Serves 4

1 pound bananas
1 cup dark rum

Ice

- ◆ Peel the bananas. Place the bananas and the rum in a food processor. Blend until smooth.
- ◆ Serve in glasses over crushed ice.

STRAWBERRY DAIQUIRIS

Serves 4

1 quart strawberries   Ice
1 cup dark rum

- ♦ In a food processor place washed strawberries and rum. Blend until smooth.
- ♦ Serve in glasses over crushed ice.

SANGRIA

We like to serve Sangria on hot summer nights with gazpacho and other highly seasoned foods.

1 whole orange   ½ cup sugar
1 lemon   1 quart club soda
2 fifths red wine

- ♦ Slice the orange and lemons.
- ♦ Put the red wine, lemon and orange slices, and sugar in a pitcher.
- ♦ Cool for at least four hours.
- ♦ Pour in the club soda.
- ♦ Ginger ale can be substituted for the club soda, but do not use sugar if using this.

WASSAIL WITH ALE

Makes about 16 cups

3 12 ounce bottles ale   ¼ teaspoon ginger
3 cups dark rum   1 orange, sliced
2/3 cup sugar

- ♦ In a pot combine the sugar, ginger, ale and rum, bringing to a boil. Simmer for 15 minutes.
- ♦ Pour into a punch bowl. Float orange slices on top.

APPLEJACK WASSAIL

1 gallon sweet or hard cider
10 2 inch cinnamon sticks
1 tablespoon allspice

½ cup fresh lemon juice
2 cups sugar (less can be used)
¼ bottle Applejack or Calvados

- Heat together all ingredients, except the Applejack, until the mixture comes to a boil. Simmer for 15 minutes.
- Add the Applejack and serve hot in large bowl.
- Decorate with apple slices.
- Makes about 26 6 ounce cups.

Now Let Us Praise Fried Pies

MINT JULEPS

Even though mint juleps are associated with the Kentucky Derby, they can be served on other occasions.

The mint julep was first served at Old White Springs in Virginia in 1858. The drink was made with brandy, cut loaf sugar, limestone water, crushed ice and mountain mint.

For one drink

4 mint leaves
1½ teaspoons sugar
1 tablespoon water

4 ounces bourbon
Crushed ice

- Place the mint, sugar and water in a silver mint julep cup.
- Crush the mint and let the sugar dissolve. Add ice and pour bourbon over this.

HOT COFFEE WITH RUM

1 cup rum
4 cups hot coffee

½ cup cream, whipped

- Evenly divide the coffee and rum among 4 mugs.
- Top with whipped cream.

CHAMPAGNE PUNCH

Serves about 25 cups

2 bottles champagne
1 cup brandy
2 bottles Chardonnay

1 pound strawberries
1 round mold ice

- ♦ Into a punch bowl pour the wine, brandy and strawberries.
- ♦ Just before serving add champagne and ice mold.
- ♦ Serve in punch cups.

BRANDY ALEXANDER

The first time I ever had a Brandy Alexander was at my uncle's farm in Fallston, Maryland, making them with vanilla ice cream instead of whipped cream! I spent the summer on Nantucket with my grandmother. My sister and I offered to take her down to the Jared Coffin House for an evening of sea chanteys and a drink. She asked what she should have to drink. We suggested a Brandy Alexander. She had two and we almost had to carry her home.

½ pint heavy cream
8 ounces brandy

8 ounces crème de cacao
Nutmeg

- ♦ Pour the cream, brandy and crème de cacao into a cocktail shaker with crushed ice.
- ♦ Shake well and strain into cocktail glasses. Sprinkle with nutmeg.

MARGUERITA

Coarse salt
10 ounces tequila
¼ cup fresh lime juice

2 ounces Triple Sec
Lime slices

- ♦ Cut the lime in half and rub with one half the rim of two glasses, and then dip the glasses into the salt.
- ♦ Pour the tequila, triple sec and lime juice into a cocktail shaker. Shake well. Serve in glasses over crushed ice and with lemon slice.

SOUPS

Clam Chowder

CRAB SOUP

Serves 6-8

1 pound crab meat	1 cup corn
1 pound chicken, cut-up	1 cup peas
3 quarts water	1 cup potatoes
1 large onion, chopped	1 teaspoon salt
3 stalks celery, chopped	¼ teaspoon pepper
1 15 ounce can tomatoes	½ teaspoon cayenne

- Put the water and chicken in a large pot. Cover and simmer over low heat for one hour.
- Peel and chop the potatoes.
- Add the vegetables and seasonings to the pot. Cover and simmer for 45 minutes.
- Add crab meat and simmer for 15 minutes.
- Serve in individual bowls.

CREAM OF CRAB SOUP

Serves 8

1 pound crab meat	1 cup chicken stock
1 small onion, chopped	4 tablespoons flour
2 tablespoons butter	½ cup sherry
1 quart cream or half and half	Salt and pepper
Parsley	

- Saute the onion in butter until transparent. Stir in flour.
- Add the chicken stock and slowly pour in the cream until thickened. Add salt and pepper.
- Serve soup in bowls, garnished with parsley.
- Put the sherry in a pitcher and let guests take desired amount.

OYSTER STEW

This is traditionally served Thanksgiving, Christmas and/or New Year's Eve.

Serves 4-6

1 quart oysters with liquor
1 quart half and half
½ stick butter

Salt and pepper to taste
Paprika

- Cook oysters in liquor for about 5 minutes.
- Add half and half, butter, salt and pepper.
- Serve in a soup tureen or individual bowls. Sprinkle with paprika.

GAZPACHO

Serves 8

8 cups tomatoes, peeled
1 green pepper, chopped
1 large onion, chopped
1 large cucumber, peeled
2 cloves garlic, peeled

3 tablespoons olive oil
Salt and pepper to taste
½ teaspoon cayenne
1 tsp. Worcestershire sauce
Croutons

- Put all ingredients, except croutons, in food processor. Blend until smooth.
- Serve in bowls topped with croutons.

EASY GAZPACHO

1 large can V8 juice
1 large pepper, chopped
1 large onion, chopped
1 large cucumber, peeled
2 cloves garlic

3 tablespoons olive oil
1 tsp. Worcestershire sauce
½ teaspoon cayenne
Croutons

- Place all ingredients, except croutons, in food processor until well blended.
- Serve in bowls with croutons.

CLAM CHOWDER

This is good served with Portuguese or sourdough bread and a green salad.

Serves 4-6

2 dozen hard shell clams
1 quart half and half
1 large onion, chopped
6 slices bacon

¼ teaspoon pepper
½ teaspoon salt
2 cups diced potatoes
½ stick butter

- Preheat oven to 350°.
- Place clams on cookie sheet. Bake until clams just open.
- Reserve the clam broth and put the clams in a large pot.
- Fry bacon in a skillet. Remove bacon and saute onions in bacon fat.
- Boil potatoes until tender.
- To the clam pot add the potatoes, onions, half and half, clam broth, salt and pepper, and last the bacon.
- Simmer until warm, but do not let boil. Just before serving add butter. Serve in bowls.

WATERCRESS SOUP

Serves 4

2 bunches watercress
4 tablespoons butter
1 cup onion, chopped
2 cup leeks, chopped
4 potatoes, peeled and sliced

3 cups chicken stock
Salt and pepper to taste
1 cup milk
1 cup heavy cream

- Melt 1 tablespoon butter in large saucepan. Add onion, leeks and chopped watercress and cook for about five minutes.
- Add sliced potatoes and stock. Bring to boil and let simmer for one hour. Remove from heat. Let cool.
- Puree the soup in a food processor.
- Return the puree to the pot and add milk, cream and salt and pepper to taste. Slowly stir in 3 tablespoons butter. Do not boil.
- This can be served hot or cold in bowls. Garnish with extra watercress.

RON'S VICHYSSOISE

Serves 6-8

3 cups peeled sliced potatoes
3 cups sliced leeks
1½ quarts chicken stock

Salt and white pepper to taste
1 cup heavy cream
Chives, minced

- ◆ Simmer potatoes and leeks in chicken broth for 45 minutes.
- ◆ Puree in blender. Cool.
- ◆ Stir in cream. Season to taste.
- ◆ Serve in bowls and garnish with minced chives.

BROCCOLI SOUP

Serves 6

2 cups cooked broccoli
1 medium onion, chopped
1 large carrot, sliced
1 celery stalk, sliced
1 clove garlic, minced

¼ cup butter
4 cups chicken stock
2 cups cream
Salt and pepper to season
Chives

- ◆ Saute carrot, onion, sliced celery and garlic in butter. Place in food processor and add broccoli.
- ◆ Pour into a bowl and stir in stock and cream.
- ◆ Serve chilled in bowls and garnish with chives.

WONTON SOUP

1 package wonton wrappers
½ pound chicken, cooked
1 can water chestnuts
¼ cup soy sauce

2 tablespoons dry Sherry
4 scallions
4 cups chicken broth

- ◆ In a food processor put the chicken, water chestnuts, soy sauce, Sherry and 3 scallions. Process until well blended.
- ◆ Lay out the wonton wrappers and place a spoonful of the meat mixture on each wrapper. Fold the corners and seal with water.
- ◆ Finely chop the other scallion and place in boiling chicken broth in a saucepan. Add wonton to broth and cook for 2 minutes.

COLD CUCUMBER SOUP

8 servings

¼ cup butter
4 cucumbers, peeled and sliced
1 large leek, minced
1 large celery heart, minced

8 cups chicken broth
1 cup heavy cream
Salt and pepper to taste
¼ cup chopped chives

- Melt butter in a heavy saucepan.
- Add cucumbers, leek, and celery and cook until tender.
- Add chicken broth and bring to boil. Cook for 30 minutes. Let cool.
- Place in food processor.
- Then put back into saucepan, adding cream. Bring to a boil.
- Refrigerate. Serve cold in bowls and garnish with chives.

CREAM OF PEA SOUP

Serves 4-6

Broth

4 cups water
1 carrot
1 celery stalk

1 leek
1 tablespoon fresh parsley
1 bay leaf

- Place all ingredients in pot, bring to boil and then simmer for 30 minutes. Strain and reserve liquid as the broth.

½ cup onion, chopped
2 cups shelled peas

2 tablespoons butter
½ cup heavy cream

- Saute onion in butter and add peas. Add broth and simmer for 20 minutes.
- Add cream. Remove from heat and let cool.
- Serve in individual bowls with parsley or fresh mint as garnish.
- For a spicier flavor add 2 teaspoons curry.

CHILLED CANTALOUPE SOUP

Serves 4-6

1 large cantaloupe
½ teaspoon cinnamon
Juice of 1 lime

2 cups orange juice
Mint

- ◆ Place the pulp of the cantaloupe and cinnamon in food processor.
- ◆ Combine lime and orange juices. Combine with cantaloupe puree.
- ◆ Chill in a bowl. Serve in bowls with mint leaves as garnish.

Winter's Repast

Ron's Onion Soup
French Bread
Mixed Green Salad
Fruit and Cheese

RON'S ONION SOUP

Serves 8

5 cups onions, thinly sliced
3 tablespoons butter
1 tablespoon olive oil
1 teaspoon salt
¼ teaspoon sugar
3 tablespoons flour

2 quarts boiling beef broth
½ cup dry white wine
Salt and pepper
French bread, sliced and toasted
Parmesan cheese

- ◆ Cook onions in butter and olive oil in covered pan for 15 minutes, stirring occasionally. Uncover, raise heat and stir.
- ◆ Add salt and sugar. Cook 30-40 minutes until onions are a deep golden brown. Stir in flour.
- ◆ Take off burner and add beef broth, wine, salt and pepper. Simmer partially covered for 30-40 minutes.
- ◆ Pour into a soup tureen or cups over rounds of toasted French bread.
- ◆ Pass freshly grated parmesan cheese.

DILL SOUP

Serves 6

2 or more large stems dill with
leaves, flower and stem
1 pound fresh green beans
1 quart water
1 small onion, chopped
1 tablespoon olive oil

¼ cup flour
2 cups beef stock
1 cup sour cream
2 tablespoons white wine
vinegar

- Finely chop the dill. Save some for garnish.
- Cook the beans with the dill in the quart of water until soft.
- Saute onion in the oil, add flour and stir till smooth and thickened.
- Add beef stock to bean stock.
- Cool. Add vinegar and sour cream.
- Serve chilled, garnished with dill.

CORN CHOWDER

Serves 6

2 cups fresh corn
1 medium onion, chopped
1 cup raw potato, sliced
3 cups boiling water
4 slices bacon
Salt and pepper to taste

1 tablespoon sugar
1 cup cream
1 cup milk
2 egg yolks, beaten
3 tablespoons butter
Parsley or chives

- Fry the bacon in a large skillet and reserve 1 tablespoon of the bacon fat.
- Crumble the bacon back in the skillet.
- Saute the onion and potato with the bacon. Stir in the corn.
- Add boiling water, sugar and salt and pepper. Simmer for 30 minutes.
- Stir in cream and milk.
- Just before serving, stir in egg yolks and butter
- Serve in bowls with parsley or chives for garnish.
- Adding ¼ cup chopped red pepper adds color to the soup.
- Adding ½ teaspoon cayenne makes for a spicier chowder.

CREAM OF MUSHROOM SOUP

Serves 4-6

1 pound mushrooms, sliced
½ stick butter
1 small onion, chopped
¼ cup flour
3 cups chicken stock

1 cup heavy cream
Salt and pepper to taste
2 tablespoons Sherry

- ◆ Melt the butter in a large pot. Add the onion and cook until transparent. Add the mushrooms and cook for 4 minutes.
- ◆ Stir in flour and slowly add the chicken stock. Bring to a boil. Reduce heat and simmer for 5 minutes. Stir in the cream, salt, pepper, and Sherry.

HAM AND BEAN SOUP

Serves 6-8

1 ham bone with meat
2 quarts water
1 large onion, chopped
1 cup celery, chopped

2 bay leaves
Salt and pepper
1 pound navy beans

- ◆ Cover the ham bone with water in a large pot. Add the beans, which have been soaked overnight, onion, celery, bay leaves, salt and pepper. Bring to a boil. Simmer for 2 hours.

CREAM OF TOMATO SOUP

6 ripe large tomatoes
1 small onion, diced
1 clove garlic, chopped
2 sprigs fresh dill

2 cups chicken stock
2 cups heavy cream
Salt and pepper to taste

- ◆ Core and peel the tomatoes. Put into a large pot. Add the onion, garlic, salt, pepper, dill, and chicken stock. Cover and simmer for ½ hour.
- ◆ Transfer to a food processor and blend together. Remove and pour into a soup tureen. Add cream. Chill and serve garnished with dill.

ASPARAGUS SOUP

Serves 6

2 pounds asparagus
½ stick butter
1 small onion, chopped
2 cloves garlic, crushed
¼ cup flour

3 cups chicken stock
1 cup heavy cream
Salt and pepper to taste
Lemon slices

- Cut the asparagus into 2 inch pieces. In a boiling pot of water blanche asparagus for 4 minutes. Reserve the asparagus tips.
- Melt the butter in a large pot and saute the onions and garlic until transparent.
- Stir in the flour and slowly add the chicken broth.
- Add the asparagus (not the tips) and bring to a boil. Simmer for 20-30 minutes. Remove from the heat.
- Puree the asparagus mixture in a food processor.
- Return to the pot and add the cream and asparagus tips.
- Ladle into bowls or a soup tureen. Garnish with lemon slices.

CARROT SOUP

Serves 6

1 stick butter
8 cups carrots, sliced
1 cup onion, chopped
6 cups chicken stock

1 cup cream
Salt and pepper
½ cup vermouth
Parsley

- Melt the butter in a saucepan and saute the carrots over low heat for 5 minutes.
- Add the onion and saute for 4 minutes more.
- Stir in stock and cream. Simmer for 35 minutes.
- Add vermouth, salt and pepper.
- Pour the mixture into a food processor and blend until smooth.
- Return to the saucepan and reheat. Garnish with parsley.
- This can also be served cold.

SEAFOOD

Chesapeake Bay Oysters

The Chesapeake Bay spans about 64,000 miles and is mainly located in Maryland. However Delaware and Virginia are included in this book as well. The Algonquin Indians called it "Chesepiooc" which means "Great Shell Bay".

The region is world famous for crabs, oysters, rockfish and shad, especially the roe. Fishing for shad on the Bay was banned for a time. Projects are now underway to open the many dams so that they can swim back up the rivers to spawn.

Oysters have been around for millions of years. The oysters produce by spawning. The spawning period is from June until September. Oysters grow to be about 3 inches in three years.

Captain Frederick Marryat visited the United States in 1837 and wrote in "A Diary of America" that "Oysters are very plentiful, very large, and to an English palate, rather insipid. As the Americans assert that the English and French oysters taste of copper, and that they therefore cannot eat them, I presume they do, and that's the reason we do like the American oysters, copper being better than no flavor at all".

However, Americans thought very differently about this and Baltimore and Crisfield were to become the oyster capitals of the U.S. Oyster canning began in Baltimore in 1840. In 1891 15 million bushels of oysters were harvested from the Bay and about 1500 workboats operated on the Bay. From the 1920s to 1970s the oyster catch averaged 15 million pounds a year. Many years later the supply of oysters was severely depleted, but thanks to some special programs, seed beds have helped them make a comeback.

Waterman is probably an English term for the hard working fishermen of the Chesapeake. Oystermen are tongers or dredgers "drudgers" Tongs have been around since c 1700. They look like a double rake with a basket. Patent tongs were invented by Charles L. Marsh, a blacksmith on the Patuxent River, in 1887. These operated remotely with a winch, and could get into deeper places with less effort. A hydraulic tong was patented in 1958 by William Barrett and T. Rayner Wilson.

A patent tonger is a vessel that uses hydraulically powered oyster tongs to retrieve the oysters. Hand tongers do the same thing with muscle powered rake shafts. The season is September 15-March 31.

The bugeye is a two-masted schooner descended from the canoe, and was used for oystering in shallow waters, beginning in the 1860s. The boats were made from 7 logs. Almost 600 bugeyes were produced, about half built near Crisfield. Sadly only a few of these remain on the Bay, mainly used now as pleasure boats.

The pungy (pongee or oyster boat) was a bit larger and carried topmasts. The schooner rigs were descended from the Baltimore clippers and were used for dredging oysters.

The scow is a flat-bottomed sailing craft with a square bow and stern. The boats were later rigged as schooners and sloops. They hauled grain, fish and salt. Hunters used them as houseboats.

Sloops in the U.S. date back to when Captain John Smith first explored the Chesapeake Bay in this type of vessel. During the Revolution and War of 1812 sloops plied the waters of the Chesapeake and were noted for their speed against much larger British ships. The ships were also used for trading and in the mid 1800s to transport oysters. Some were used as dredgers for oystering and others as 'buy boats". These were later to be replaced by the skipjack.

The skipjack is an exclusive Chesapeake design from the old Indian dug-out sailing canoes. They were first used in the 1890's to dredge oysters. A dredge is dragged over the oyster beds (bars) to loosen them with a dredge bag attached to catch them.

The skipjack has a single raked mast and centerboard. Skipjacks dredge by law for oysters under sail Wednesday through Friday and use of a push boat on Mondays and Tuesdays. Only about 30 skipjacks are left. In November 1999 the State of Maryland announced a special program to help fund the restoration and upkeep of these boats. The skipjack is the official boat of Maryland.

Crabbing became a major industry on the Bay in the 1870's, reaching its peak in 1920 with 50 million pounds. The best season for crabs is in the spring. The Maryland blue crab is native to the Chesapeake Bay and the Eastern Coast of the United States. Crabbers trap crabs by using trotlines, which are long baited lines that run along the Bay, creek or river's bottom and are anchored at each end. Baited crab pots are also employed.

The Blue Crab's Latin name means "Beautiful Swimmer". Male crabs are called "jimmies', and female "sooks". Blue crabs molt (or shed) their shells to increase their size, and during this stage the crab has a soft shell, thus soft-shell crabs. Crabbers know when a crab is about to molt by markings on their bodies. They are then called "peelers" and are put in holding tanks. Once they have shed their shells they are sold as soft-shell crabs. Lump crab meat is the largest and most expensive type of crab meat.

Hard-shell clams and maninose (soft clams) are found in the Bay. Maninose are also called steamers and have a longer, narrower shell than hard-shell crabs.

Rockfish is the official fish of the State of Maryland. Rockfish is a striped bass and is delicious served sauteed, stuffed, served with white sauce, or whatever method you want to try.

CRAB CAKES

4 crab cakes

1 pound crab meat	1 teaspoon mustard
2 tablespoons bread crumbs	2 tablespoons mayonnaise
1 egg	Dash of Old Bay Seasoning
1 tsp. Worcestershire sauce	Butter

- With a fork carefully combine the ingredients in a bowl.
- Shape into cakes. Saute in butter until brown on each side.
- Serve on sourdough rolls with tartar sauce and lemon

Summer Night Repast

Steamed Crabs
Corn on the Cob
Cole Slaw
Sliced Tomatoes
Corn Relish
Herb Bread
Watermelon
Beer

STEAMED CRABS

Serves 6-8

2 dozen crabs
2 cans beer

2 cups vinegar
½ cup Old Bay Seasoning

- ◆ Place the crabs in a large pot with the beer, vinegar and Old Bay Seasoning. Steam 20-30 minutes or until crabs are red.
- ◆ Serve crabs hot outside on a table covered with newspapers or brown paper.
- ◆ Have plenty of paper napkins, mallets, and crab picks available.
- ◆ To pick a crab, flip the crab over, open the apron and then the top shell.
- ◆ Discard the gills and devil.
- ◆ Break the crab in half. Pull the legs and claws off.
- ◆ Suck the meat out of the legs and save the claws.
- ◆ With a paring knife split each half of the crab and take the meat out. Break the claws in half with a mallet.
- ◆ Just keep eating and what a feast you'll have, though crab picking does take some practice.

SOFT-SHELL CRABS ALMONDINE

Serves 4

12 soft-shell crabs
½ cup flour

¼ cup butter
½ cup toasted almonds

- Rinse the crabs in cold water. Cut out the eyes and mouth with a paring knife. Turn over and remove the apron. Fold back the pointed ends on the shell and remove the spongy gills. Dry the crabs with paper towels.
- Dredge the crabs in the flour.
- Heat the butter in a skillet and saute the crabs about 3 minutes to a side.
- Place on a platter and sprinkle with the almonds. Serve immediately.
- If preferred the crabs can be placed in a broiling pan and broiled for 3-5 minutes.

FILET OF SOLE WITH CRAB MEAT

Serves 6-8

3 pounds filet of sole
2 cups dry white wine
¼ cup fresh parsley
½ lb. mushrooms, chopped
¼ cup butter
¼ cup flour

1 cup grated Gruyere cheese
¼ cup sherry
½ pound crab meat
½ cup heavy cream
Salt and pepper

- Preheat oven to 400°.
- Cook the wine over low heat until reduced by ½ in a saucepan. Add the parsley. Saute the mushrooms in 2 tablespoons butter.
- In a separate saucepan melt the remaining butter, stir in the flour and then wine until thickened. Add the mushrooms, ½ cup cheese, sherry, crab meat and cream.
- Spread half the sauce in a large flat baking dish. Place the filet of sole on top and add rest of crab mixture and cheese. Top with the rest of the sauce.
- Bake for 15 minutes and then put under broiler until golden.
- Serve on a platter garnished with lemon slices and parsley.

FRIED SOFT-SHELL CRABS

Serves 4

12 soft-shell crabs	1 tsp. Old Bay Seasoning
½ cup flour	Oil

- ◆ Combine the flour and seasoning. Dredge the crabs in the flour.
- ◆ Heat the oil in a skillet. Fry the crabs until browned on both sides.
- ◆ Place on a platter. Serve with lemon slices and tartar sauce.

DEVILED CRAB

Serves 4

1 pound crab meat	¼ teaspoon cayenne
½ stick butter	¼ cup bread crumbs
¼ cup green onion, chopped	½ cup cream
2 tablespoons flour	2 hard cooked eggs
1 teaspoon Dijon mustard	2 tablespoons fresh parsley
1 tsp. Worcestershire sauce	

- ◆ Preheat the oven to 350°.
- ◆ Melt the butter in a saucepan and add the onions, sauteing them for about 2 minutes until tender.
- ◆ Remove from the heat and stir in the flour, mustard, cream, Worcestershire sauce, and cayenne. Return to the heat and cook until thickened.
- ◆ Put the crab meat, eggs and parsley in a casserole.
- ◆ Pour the cream sauce over the top and gently blend in with the crab.
- ◆ Bake 25-30 minutes, until browned on top.

CRAB IMPERIAL

Serves 6-8

2 pounds crab meat	2 eggs
1 tablespoon Dijon mustard	Juice of ½ lemon
1 cup mayonnaise	1 tsp. Worcestershire sauce
1 teaspoon salt	¼ teaspoon cayenne
1 green pepper, chopped	¼ teaspoon pepper

- Combine all the ingredients except crab meat in a bowl. This can be covered and refrigerated until ready to use.
- Place the ingredients in a casserole and gently add crab meat.
- Top with just a small amount of mayonnaise.
- Bake at 350° for 15 minutes.
- Sprinkle with paprika before serving.

CRAB GUMBO

Serves 6

1½ pounds crab meat	1 bay leaf
1 medium onion, chopped	1 teaspoon salt
1 stalk celery, chopped	½ teaspoon thyme
2 cloves garlic, crushed	½ teaspoon cayenne
½ stick butter	Pepper
1 large can whole tomatoes	3 cups cooked rice
½ pound okra, trimmed	

- In a large pot cook the okra, onion and celery in butter until tender.
- Then add the garlic, tomatoes, and spices. Simmer for one hour.
- Add the crab meat.
- Serve over rice

OYSTERS ROCKEFELLER

We like to serve this as an hors d'oeuvre on Christmas day.

1 quart oysters
2 10 ounce packages chopped spinach
Juice of 1 lemon

1 small onion, chopped
½ teaspoon Tabasco sauce
Grated cheese

- ◆ Defrost the spinach in a colander. Combine spinach in a bowl with the onion, lemon juice and Tabasco sauce.
- ◆ Open the oysters and discard one shell. Place the oysters in a large baking dish.
- ◆ Spread the spinach mixture on the tops of the oysters. Sprinkle with grated cheese.
- ◆ Bake at 400° for about ten minutes.

FRIED OYSTERS

Serves 4-6

1 quart oysters
1 cup flour

Salt and pepper
Oil

- ◆ In a bowl combine the flour and salt and pepper.
- ◆ Drain the liquor from the oysters.
- ◆ Dredge the oysters in the flour. Be careful to keep the oysters separate, as they are very delicate.
- ◆ Pour oil into a skillet. Heat until bubbling hot.
- ◆ Fry the oysters until browned on both sides, about 5 minutes each side.
- ◆ Serve with seafood sauce, tartar sauce, or lemon slices.

OYSTER-BEEF PIE

1 9 inch pie crust
1 pound sirloin
1 pint oysters
¼ cup butter, melted

¼ cup flour
1 shallot, chopped
Salt and pepper to taste
1 cup beef stock

- ◆ Preheat oven to 425°.
- ◆ Pound the steak until thin and cut into strips to hold ½ an oyster.
- ◆ Cut the oysters in half. Roll the steak around the oyster and then dip in melted butter. Dredge in flour.
- ◆ Place the rolls in the pan very tightly. Fill the pan with stock to which the shallot has been added.
- ◆ Cover the oyster rolls and stock with the pie crust. Cut a hole in the top to vent the steam.
- ◆ Place in the oven and bake for 15 minutes at 425°.
- ◆ Lower oven temperature to 350° and bake for 45 minutes or until top is browned.

OYSTER FRITTERS

1 quart oysters
1 cup flour
1 teaspoon baking powder
2 eggs
1 teaspoon salt

¼ teaspoon pepper
1 cup milk
Oil
Tartar or seafood sauce

- ◆ Combine the flour, baking powder, salt and pepper in a bowl.
- ◆ In another bowl beat together the eggs and milk. Stir in dry ingredients.
- ◆ Stir the oysters into the batter.
- ◆ Pour about 1 inch oil into a skillet. Heat until bubbly.
- ◆ Using a large spoon drop about 3 oysters and batter into the oil. Fry until golden brown on each side. Remove and put on paper towels. Keep warm in a 200° oven.
- ◆ Serve with tartar or seafood sauce.

SCALLOPED OYSTERS

1 quart shucked oysters
¼ cup onion, chopped
1 stick butter, melted
1 teaspoon salt
1 tablespoon lemon juice

1 tsp. Worcestershire sauce
1 Tbls. parsley, chopped
2 cups crumbled Ritz crackers
¼ cup cream
¼ cup milk

- ◆ Preheat oven to 400°.
- ◆ Drain the oysters and reserve the liquor.
- ◆ Melt the butter in a skillet and saute the onions.
- ◆ Add salt, lemon juice, Worcestershire sauce, parsley and cracker crumbs. Mix well.
- ◆ In a greased casserole layer crumbs and oysters.
- ◆ Add oyster liquor, cream and the milk.
- ◆ Bake 25 minutes.

SCALLOPED OYSTER CASSEROLE

Serves 4

1 pint oysters
2 cups coarse cracker crumbs
1 stick butter, melted

¼ cup grated cheddar cheese
Half and half

- ◆ Preheat oven to 350°.
- ◆ Drain the oysters and reserve the liquor.
- ◆ Combine the crumbs and butter. Spread 1/3 of the crumbs in the bottom of a small casserole. Cover with ½ of the oysters. Sprinkle with cheese. Add 1/3 crumbs. Add remaining oysters.
- ◆ Add enough half and half to the oyster liquor to make 1 cup. Sprinkle with rest of the crumbs.
- ◆ Bake for 30-40 minutes until brown and bubbling.

CLAMS IN WHITE WINE

Serves 6

6 pounds clams
3 cloves garlic, crushed
3 cups dry white wine

¼ cup parsley, chopped
1 pound Linguine

- In a large kettle place the clams, garlic and white wine. Bring to a boil. Cover the pan until the clams open.
- Cook the linguine according the directions.
- Pour the clams and broth into a tureen or separate bowls over the linguine and garnish with the parsley.

FRIED CLAMS

The Chesapeake Bay has two types of clams - hard- and soft-shell or maninose.

Serves 6

6 cups shucked clams
4 eggs, beaten
1 cup milk
1 teaspoon salt
1 cup flour

1 cup cornmeal
1 teaspoon salt
½ teaspoon pepper
Oil

- In a bowl beat together the eggs and milk.
- In another bowl combine the flour, cornmeal and salt and pepper.
- Dredge the clams separately in the milk mixture and then the flour.
- Heat the oil in a skillet.
- Fry the clams for 1 minute and take out with a slotted spoon.
- Place on paper towels.
- Serve on a platter with tartar sauce, seafood sauce or lemon slices.

BAKED SHAD ROE

Shad roe are a delicacy found during the spring.

Serves 4

2 pounds shad roe
¼ cup softened butter
4 slices bacon, cooked and broken into small pieces

2 tablespoons parsley
1 tablespoon dill
2 tablespoons dry Vermouth

- On baking sheet place aluminum foil (enough so it can enclose the roe).
- Spread the foil with the butter, and then roe. Sprinkle with dill, parsley, bacon and vermouth.
- Bake at 400° for 25 minutes.

BAKED SHAD

Serves 4

2 pounds shad filet
1 cup bread crumbs
¼ cup parsley, chopped
¼ cup onion, chopped

¼ cup butter, melted
¼ cup dry white wine
Salt and pepper

- Preheat oven to 350°.
- In a bowl mix together the bread crumbs, parsley, onion, salt and pepper.
- Place the filets in a baking dish.
- Top with bread crumb mixture.
- Pour butter and wine over shad. Bake 30 minutes.
- Shad can also be baked in cream, but do not use the bread crumbs and white wine.
- Bake the shad with the parsley, onion and butter for 20 minutes.
- Then pour the cream over the shad and bake for 10 more minutes.
- Garnish with chopped parsley.

STUFFED ROCKFISH

Serves 6

3 pounds rockfish filet
½ cup butter
1 cup mushrooms, chopped
1 tomato, peeled and chopped
1 tablespoon chives, chopped

¼ cup parsley, chopped
¾ cup fresh bread crumbs
Salt and pepper
¼ cup lemon juice
½ cup dry white wine

♦ Preheat oven to 400°.
♦ In a skillet heat half the butter and saute onion until transparent.
♦ Add the mushrooms and saute until tender.
♦ Add the tomato and cook for 10 minutes.
♦ Add the chives, parsley, bread crumbs, salt and pepper.
♦ Stuff the fish with the stuffing. Close fish with skewers.
♦ Place the fish in a baking dish and sprinkle with lemon juice and wine.
♦ Dot with remaining butter.
♦ Bake for 30-40 minutes, until tender when tested with a fork.
♦ Serve on a platter and garnish with parsley and lemon slices.

BROILED ROCKFISH

Serves 6

3 pounds rockfish filets
½ cup Vermouth
Juice of one lemon

½ stick butter, melted
Parsley
Lemon slices

♦ Preheat the oven broiler.
♦ Mix together the Vermouth and lemon juice in a bowl.
♦ Place the rockfish in a baking dish.
♦ Pour the Vermouth and lemon over the rockfish, then the butter.
♦ Broil under the broiler until the fish is just slightly browned.
♦ Place on a platter and garnish with the lemon slices and parsley.

BAKED BLUEFISH

Serves 6

3 pounds bluefish filets
¼ cup olive oil
1 cup tomatoes, chopped
½ cup onions, chopped
¼ cup parsley, chopped
4 cloves garlic, crushed

2 stalks celery, chopped
Juice of 1 lemon
1 cup dry white wine
3 bay leaves
Salt and pepper

- ◆ Preheat oven to 375°.
- ◆ In a skillet heat the oil and add the onions, celery, and garlic. Saute until tender.
- ◆ Add the tomatoes, wine, bay leaves, and lemon juice. Simmer for 30 minutes. Season with salt and pepper.
- ◆ In a large baking dish place the fish filets. Pour the sauce over the filets. Bake for 30 minutes.

GUMBO

Serves 6-8

2 pounds shrimp, raw, shelled and deveined
1 pound sweet Italian sausage
½ cup butter
½ cup flour
1 medium onion, chopped
½ cup celery, chopped
2 cloves garlic, crushed
½ cup green pepper, chopped
½ pound okra, chopped

2 cups tomato sauce
2 cups chicken stock
½ teaspoon salt
½ teaspoon pepper
½ teaspoon thyme
1 teaspoon fresh basil
½ teaspoon cayenne
½ teaspoon Tabasco
3 cups cooked rice

- ◆ In a saucepan melt the butter and add the flour, stirring until the mixture thickens and turns brown, but not burned.
- ◆ Stir in the onion, celery, pepper, garlic and okra. Heat until the vegetables are tender.
- ◆ Brown the sausage in a skillet
- ◆ Add the tomato sauce, stock, herbs, sausage and shrimp.
- ◆ Bring to a boil and then simmer for one hour. Serve over rice.

SEAFOOD AU GRATIN

Serves 6-8

2½ pounds rockfish
1 pound scallops
3 cups water
½ small onion, sliced
½ small onion, minced
½ lemon, sliced

1 tablespoon fresh basil
2 tablespoons butter
¼ cup green pepper, chopped
½ lb. mushrooms, sliced
¼ cup bread crumbs

♦ Boil the lemon and ½ sliced onion in the water.
♦ Add the basil and cook for 5 minutes.
♦ Add the rockfish and scallops and poach for 5 minutes.
♦ Remove and break apart the fish, reserving the liquid, but discarding the lemon and onion.
♦ In a saucepan saute the minced onion and pepper in butter, and add mushrooms.

Sauce

1 cup butter
1 cup flour
2 cups cream
2 cups fish stock
½ teaspoon dry mustard

½ cup Swiss cheese or Gruyere
¼ cup dry white wine or ¼ cup sherry
Salt and pepper

♦ Melt the butter in a saucepan and slowly add the flour.
♦ Then add the cream and stock until thickened.
♦ Add the mustard, cheese, wine, salt and pepper.
♦ Combine the fish, vegetables and sauce.
♦ Pour into a baking dish.
♦ Cover with bread crumbs.
♦ Bake for 35 minutes at 350°.

STUFFED FISH

Serves 6-8

3 pounds filet of sole or perch
½ pound crab meat
½ pound shrimp
¼ cup mushrooms, chopped

¼ cup green onion, chopped
Salt and pepper, to taste
¼ teaspoon tarragon
1 clove garlic, minced

Combine the crab meat, shrimp, mushrooms, onion, salt, pepper, tarragon and garlic in a bowl.

Sauce

1 cup milk
½ stick butter
¼ cup flour

½ cup grated cheddar cheese
¼ cup Sherry

- ◆ Melt the butter in a sauce pan. Slowly stir in the flour and then milk until thickened. Add cheese and Sherry.
- ◆ Arrange ½ of the filets in a buttered baking dish and ½ of other ingredients. Pour ½ sauce over filets. Then prepare second layer.
- ◆ Bake 350° for 30 minutes.

SHRIMP CREOLE

Serves 4

1/3 cup butter
¼ cup flour
1 pound shrimp
1 clove garlic, minced
¼ onion, chopped
2 Tbls. parsley, chopped
½ green pepper, chopped

1 cup water
1 teaspoon salt
2 bay leaves
½ cup celery
1 8 ounce can tomato sauce
½ teaspoon cayenne
2 cups cooked rice

- ◆ Melt the butter in a skillet. Add flour and stir until brown. Add the shrimp. Cook 3 minutes.
- ◆ Add the celery, onion, parsley, and pepper and cook 2 minutes.
- ◆ Add garlic and slowly add the water, and other ingredients.
- ◆ Bring to a boil. Simmer 20-30 minutes.
- ◆ Serve over rice.

ORIENTAL SALMON

Though salmon is not found in the Bay, it is very healthy for you, and something we eat about once a week. Grilling, broiling or smoking is the best way to enjoy good salmon.

Serves 6-8

3 pounds salmon filet
¼ cup soy sauce
6 garlic cloves, crushed

¼ cup fresh ginger, grated
¼ cup karo syrup or maple syrup
Juice of one lemon

♦ In a bowl mix together the soy sauce, crushed garlic, ginger, syrup and lemon juice.
♦ Put the salmon on a large platter and coat the fish with the sauce.
♦ Cover the fish and marinate at least one hour.
♦ Grill until desired doneness.
♦ Garnish with parsley and thin lemon slices.

SMOKED SALMON WITH AVOCADO

Serves 6-8

3 pounds salmon filet
3 avocados, peeled and sliced
3 jalapeno chiles, minced

Juice of 3 limes
¼ cup fresh cilantro
1 lime, sliced

♦ Smoke the salmon on a smoker for about two hours. Remove and place on a platter. Garnish with the avocado slices.
♦ In a bowl whisk together the lime juice, cilantro and chiles.
♦ Pour the sauce over the salmon.
♦ Garnish with lime slices.

FOWL

Duck Decoys

Duck and other waterfowl were once in such abundance they blackened the skies of the Chesapeake. So many were killed that in 1918 Delaware banned the sale of migratory birds.

Chickens have been raised on the Eastern Shore of Maryland and in Delaware since the 1930s and have been a major source of income for the Delmarva Peninsula.

ROAST DUCK AND MADEIRA SAUCE

Serves 4

1 duck 5-6 pounds
Kosher salt
1 apple, cored and sliced

1 orange, cut into slices
2 celery stalks, chopped
1 onion, sliced

- ◆ Preheat the oven to 350°.
- ◆ Rub the outside of the duck with salt.
- ◆ Place the apple, orange, celery and onion in the duck cavity.
- ◆ Bake the duck 20 minutes to pound, or until skin is crisp on the outside.
- ◆ Serve with wild rice accompanied by Madeira sauce.

Madeira Sauce

1 cup consomme
2 tablespoons flour
2 tablespoons butter
½ cup raisins

1 Tbls. orange rind, grated
2 cloves
¼ cup Madeira

- ◆ In a saucepan combine the Madeira, raisins, orange rind, and cloves. Bring to a boil, then let simmer for 5 minutes. Remove from heat. Discard the cloves.
- ◆ Remove the duck to a platter and add 1 cup consomme to the pan. Scrap the side of the pan to loosen pan drippings. Stir in butter and then flour until thickened.
- ◆ Add the Madeira, raisins and orange rind.

ROAST DUCK

Serves 10-12

2 large ducks, quartered
½ cup white wine
1/3 cup olive oil
1 tablespoon onion, grated

1 clove garlic, crushed
1 tablespoon paprika
1 Tbls. Worcestershire sauce
Salt and pepper

- Preheat the oven to 500°.
- Arrange the duck quarters in a casserole dish.
- Combine the other ingredients and brush over the duck.
- Turn the oven back to 350°.
- Roast duck about one hour or until browned and tender.

CHICKEN WITH CHIPPED BEEF

Serves 6-8

8 chicken breasts
8 slices of bacon

8 ounces chipped beef

- Line a casserole with the chipped beef.
- Wrap bacon slices around each chicken breast. Place the chicken on chipped beef.

Sauce

1 stick butter
2 cups half and half

½ cup flour
1 cup sour cream

- Melt the butter in saucepan. Stir in the flour, and then slowly stir in the half and half. When this is thickened, stir in the sour cream.
- Pour the sauce over the chicken.
- Bake covered for 1 hour in 350° oven.

Quick and Easy Dinner Party

Easy Chicken
Basmati Rice
Watercress Salad
Cornbread
Apple Brown Betty

EASY CHICKEN

Serves 8

This is very good served with cranberry chutney, or any other types of chutneys.

8 chicken breasts	2 teaspoons fine herbs
½ cup parmesan cheese	½ stick butter
½ cup bread crumbs	

- ◆ Mix the cheese, crumbs and fine herbs in a bowl.
- ◆ Roll the breasts in the crumb mixture and place in a baking dish. Cover with melted butter.
- ◆ Bake 350° for 45 minutes.

BARBECUED CHICKEN

The best barbecue sauce comes not from Maryland, but from Ridgewood Restaurant in Bluff City, Tennessee. However you can make your own, or buy the sauce already prepared.

Serves 6

6 chicken breasts, boned	1 cup barbecue sauce

- ◆ Coat chicken with barbecue sauce. Grill on barbecue about 10 minutes per side.

BROCCOLI DIVAN

Serves 6-8

2 pounds broccoli, cooked and cut into pieces

3 cups cooked chicken
Sauce, recipe follows

♦ Line the casserole with the broccoli and top with the chicken.

Sauce

½ stick butter
¼ cup flour
1 cup milk
½ cup cream

¼ teaspoon nutmeg
Salt and pepper
¼ cup Gruyere cheese
¼ cup sherry

♦ Melt the butter in a saucepan.
♦ Slowly stir in the flour, then milk and cream, until thickened. Add the cheese until melted.
♦ Then add sherry, nutmeg, and salt and pepper to taste.
♦ Pour the sauce over the chicken.
♦ Bake at 350° for 30 minutes when sauce is slightly browned and bubbly.

CREAMED CHICKEN

½ cup peas or celery can be added for color.

Serves 4-6

3 cups cooked chicken
2 cups half and half
½ cup flour

½ stick butter
½ cup Sherry
3 cups cooked rice

♦ Melt the butter in a saucepan.
♦ Stir in the flour and slowly add half and half.
♦ Stir in the Sherry.
♦ Cube the chicken and add to the sauce.
♦ Serve over rice.

CHICKEN TETRAZZINI

Serves 4-6

- Use creamed chicken recipe, without rice.
- Instead saute ½ pound chopped mushrooms and ¼ cup minced onion in butter.
- In boiling pot of water cook ½ pound spaghetti.
- Mix creamed chicken, mushrooms and spaghetti in a casserole dish. Sprinkle with grated parmesan cheese.
- Bake at 350° for ½ hour, or until top is browned.

AUNT MILDRED'S CHICKEN

Serves 6

6 chicken breasts, boned   1 can mushroom soup
6 strips bacon   8 ounce carton sour cream
1 jar chipped beef

- Preheat oven to 350°.
- Roll the bacon around each breast. Line a casserole with dried beef and place the breasts on top.
- Combine the soup and sour cream. Pour over the chicken. Bake uncovered for 1½ hours.

Now Let Us Praise Fried Pies

DIJON CHICKEN

Serves 6

6 boneless chicken breasts   6 tablespoons Dijon mustard
6 tablespoons butter   ¼ cup honey

- Preheat oven to 400°.
- Place chicken in a casserole dish.
- In a bowl combine the butter, mustard and honey. Pour over the chicken.
- Bake for 30-40 minutes, until chicken is tender.

FRIED CHICKEN

Serves 6

6 chicken breasts
½ cup flour
½ teaspoon coarse salt
1 teaspoon garlic salt

1 teaspoon pepper
1 tablespoon poultry seasoning
Oil

- ♦ In a paper bag combine the flour, salt, garlic salt, pepper, and poultry seasoning. Add a chicken breast or two to bag and shake well. Shake other breasts.
- ♦ Heat oil in skillet until bubbling. Drop in chicken breasts and cook until golden brown. Turn chicken. Serve hot or cold.

CHICKEN CURRY

Lamb or pork can be substituted for the chicken.

Serves 6

3 cups cooked chicken, cubed
½ cup celery, diced
¼ cup onions, chopped
2 cups chicken broth
2 cloves garlic, crushed

1 tablespoon curry
1 tablespoon ginger, grated
½ cup apples, diced
½ cup raisins
½ cup flour

- ♦ Saute the onion and celery in 1 tablespoon butter.
- ♦ Add the garlic and chicken.
- ♦ Stir in the flour and slowly add chicken broth until thickened.
- ♦ Add the curry, apples and raisins.
- ♦ Serve over rice.

SUNDAY NIGHT CHICKEN SUPPER

Serves 8-10

1 can water chestnuts, sliced
2 packages frozen broccoli, cooked and drained
3 cooked chicken breasts, cut into small pieces
2 cans cream of mushroom soup

1 cup mayonnaise
1 tablespoon lemon juice
1 teaspoon mustard
1 teaspoon curry powder
1 cup grated cheddar cheese
½ cup fresh bread crumbs

- ◆ Combine the soup, mayonnaise, curry, lemon juice, mustard and water chestnuts in bowl.
- ◆ Layer in a casserole dish the chicken, soup mixture and cheese.
- ◆ Repeat the layer.
- ◆ Top with breadcrumbs.
- ◆ Bake at 350° for 45 minutes.

MEXICAN CHICKEN

This is a good way to use leftover chicken.

Serves 4

4 large tortillas
2 cups cooked chicken, diced
2 cups tomato sauce (salsa or something spicy is good for this)

½ cup sour cream
1 cup grated Monterey Jack cheese

- ◆ On each tortilla spread 1 tablespoon tomato sauce down center.
- ◆ Over this place ½ cup chicken, and a small amount of sour cream. Roll up the tortillas. Place in a 9x12" baking dish.
- ◆ Cover with rest of tomato sauce and sprinkle with Monterey Jack cheese. Bake at 350° for 20 minutes or until cheese bubbles.
- ◆ You can make this as spicy as you want. We usually add some green jalapenos to the chicken or tomato sauce.

ROAST CHICKEN

Most of us "Baby Boomers" grew up with roast chicken or turkey, mashed potatoes and peas as a favorite meal. Now a number of the most chic restaurants have gone back to serving this on a regular basis.

4 pound roasting chicken	1 small onion, chopped
6 slices white bread (leftover French or Italian bread can be substituted), cubed	2 tablespoons parsley
	¼ cup celery, chopped
	Salt and pepper to taste
¼ cup butter	1 Tbls. poultry seasoning

- ◆ Preheat the oven to 350°.
- ◆ Saute the onion and celery in the butter, gradually stirring in the bread cubes.
- ◆ Season with salt and pepper, poultry seasoning and parsley.
- ◆ Remove the innards from the chicken, and rinse the chicken in cold water.
- ◆ Stuff the cavity of the chicken with the bread dressing.
- ◆ Place the chicken in a roasting pan.
- ◆ Bake in oven 20 minutes to pound, until the chicken skin is browned and crisp. Remove from pan and place on a platter.
- ◆ Using the pan drippings, combine enough flour to thicken. A little water can also be added if too thick. Season with salt and pepper. Serve in a gravy boat with the chicken.

CHINESE CHICKEN

Serves 4-6

4 large chicken breasts, boned	1 tablespoon grated ginger
8 tablespoons soy sauce	2 scallions, chopped
4 teaspoons sesame oil	½ cup sesame seeds, toasted
2 tablespoons honey	3 cups cooked rice

- ◆ Combine the soy sauce, sesame oil, honey, ginger and scallions in a bowl. Add the chicken breasts. Cover and refrigerate overnight.
- ◆ In a wok heat 2 tablespoons sesame oil. Very quickly cook the chicken, adding more sesame oil if necessary.
- ◆ This is also very good with the chicken grilled on skewers.
- ◆ Sprinkle with sesame seeds. Serve over rice.

CHICKEN POT PIE

Serves 6

3 cups cooked chicken
½ cup carrots, diced
½ cup celery, chopped
½ cup onions, chopped
2 tablespoons parsley
1 clove garlic, mashed
¼ cup green onion

3 cups mashed potatoes
2 cups chicken broth
½ cup flour
2 tablespoons butter
Salt and pepper
3 tablespoons basil, chopped
¼ cup parmesan cheese

- Melt the butter in a skillet and saute the carrots, onions, celery and pepper until tender.
- Add garlic, chicken and basil. Slowly stir in flour and chicken broth until thickened.
- Place in a casserole and top with mashed potatoes and then parmesan cheese.
- Bake at 350° for ½ hour.
- Mashed sweet potatoes can be substituted for the mashed potatoes, but leave out the parmesan cheese.

CHICKEN BOURSIN

Serves 4

4 boneless chicken breasts
6 tablespoons olive oil
½ cup flour
2 eggs
½ cup parmesan cheese

1 container boursin cheese
2 scallions, finely chopped
1 clove garlic, grated
Salt and pepper to taste

- Pound the chicken breast until about ¼" thick.
- In a bowl combine the boursin, scallions, garlic, salt and pepper.
- Spread 2 tablespoons boursin mixture in the center of the chicken breast and then roll up. Dredge in the flour.
- Combine the parmesan cheese and eggs in a bowl.
- Dip the chicken breasts in mixture.
- Heat the oil in a skillet or wok and saute the chicken until browned.
- Serve over rice or noodles.

A Cold Winter's Night Dinner

Ruthie's Mexican Dip
Vegetables and Dips
George's Brunswick Stew
Jalapeno Cornbread
Mixed Greens Salad
Baked Apples

GEORGE'S BRUNSWICK STEW

Serves 20

5 pounds chicken breasts
4 slices bacon, cut up
1 large onion, sliced
½ quart chicken broth
1 green pepper
1 teaspoon salt
¼ cup parsley, chopped
1 28 ounce can tomatoes

6 potatoes, cubed
2 packages frozen lima beans
16 ounce package frozen corn
Salt and pepper to taste
1 teaspoon Tabasco sauce
Worcestershire sauce to taste
½ cup white wine

- Smoke chicken on a smoker for 2 hours. Remove from smoker and cut the chicken into bitesize pieces after cooling.
- In a large heavy pot put the chicken, bacon, onion, and salt in broth and white wine and simmer for two hours over slow heat.
- Add other ingredients and cook until thickened, approximately one hour.
- (This often takes longer than expected, so start early on preparation). Serve in separate bowls.

CHICKEN SAUSAGE BURGERS

Makes 3-4 burgers

1 pound chicken sausage
½ cup fresh breadcrumbs
2 green onions, chopped
2 tablespoons fresh dill

2 teaspoons Dijon mustard
¼ teaspoon salt
¼ teaspoon ground pepper

- Combine all the ingredients in a bowl. Shape into patties.
- Cook on grill about 6-8 minutes per side. Serve on rolls.

85

CHICKEN WITH ARTICHOKE HEARTS

Serves 6

6 boneless chicken breasts
16 oz. can artichoke hearts
¼ pound mushrooms, sliced

1 cup chicken stock
¼ cup Sherry
3 cups cooked rice

- ◆ Preheat oven to 350°.
- ◆ Place the chicken breasts in a casserole dish.
- ◆ Top with the artichoke hearts.
- ◆ Pour the chicken stock and Sherry over the chicken.
- ◆ Bake 40 minutes.
- ◆ Serve over rice.

CHICKEN IN CIDER

Serves 4-6

3½ pound whole chicken
¼ cup butter
¼ cup flour
2 tablespoons olive oil
¼ cup chopped onion

Salt and pepper
¼ cup fresh parsley, chopped
1 cup cider
2 apples, cored and sliced
½ cup heavy cream

- ◆ Cut the chicken up.
- ◆ Dredge the chicken in flour.
- ◆ Melt the butter in a skillet and add the olive oil.
- ◆ Brown the chicken, about 20 minutes to a side.
- ◆ Add the onion, herbs, apples and cider to the skillet.
- ◆ Cover and cook 45 minutes.
- ◆ Remove the chicken and add the cream to the skillet to make a sauce.
- ◆ Serve with rice and the sauce over the chicken or in separate gravy boat or pitcher.

CHICKEN LIVERS WITH
MUSHROOMS

Serves 4

2 pounds chicken livers
½ pound mushrooms
1 stick butter

¼ cup flour
1 cup cream
¼ cup dry Sherry

- ◆ In a skillet saute the mushrooms in ½ the butter.
- ◆ Remove and then saute chicken livers. Remove from skillet.
- ◆ Add flour to skillet and then cream, stirring until thickened.
- ◆ Add chicken livers, mushrooms and sherry.
- ◆ Serve over noodles.

CHICKEN LIVERS MARSALA

Serves 2

1 pound chicken livers
½ stick butter
2 slices prosciutto

¼ cup Marsala
Salt and pepper

- ◆ In a skillet heat the butter and saute the chicken livers. Add the prosciutto, salt and pepper to taste.
- ◆ Remove the liver and prosciutto from the skillet and place on a platter. Add the Marsala to the pan. Cook three minutes.
- ◆ Pour the sauce over the livers.
- ◆ Serve with rice, noodles or on toast.

Christmas Dinner

Oysters Rockefeller
Smoked Salmon
Roast Turkey or Goose
Creamed Onions
Mashed Potatoes
String Beans with Almonds
Utterly Deadly Southern Pecan Pie
Mincemeat or Pumpkin Cheesecake
Plum Pudding

ROAST TURKEY

15-20 pound turkey

♦ Preheat the oven to 350°.
♦ Rinse the turkey in cold water. Place in a large roasting pan with a cover.
♦ Remove the giblets and neck from inside turkey.
♦ Place the giblets and neck in a pan with 4 cups of water. Cook until the meat begins to fall off neck, about one hour. Remove from the pan and chop liver and heart, and take meat off neck. Reserve broth.

Sausage Dressing

6 cups white bread cubes (cornbread can be substituted)
1 medium onion, chopped
2 stalks celery, diced
Salt and pepper to season

3 Tbls. poultry seasoning
½ stick butter
¼ cup fresh parsley, chopped
1 apple, chopped
1 cup pecans
½ pound sausage

♦ In a skillet brown the sausage. Remove from the pan.
♦ Melt the butter in the skillet and saute the onion, parsley, apples, pecans, butter, and celery.
♦ Add the bread cubes.
♦ Season with salt, pepper and poultry seasoning.
♦ Stuff both cavities in the turkey with the dressing.
♦ Roast the turkey in the oven, 20-30 minutes to the pound, or until browned.
♦ Remove from oven and place turkey on serving platter.

Oyster Dressing

Use this dressing for stuffing a turkey, chicken or goose.

6 cups white bread cubes
¼ cup butter
¼ cup scallions, chopped
2 tablespoons parsley, chopped

2 tablespoons poultry seasoning
Salt and pepper
2 dozen oysters, shucked

- Melt the butter in a skillet and add the bread cubes, scallions and parsley.
- Season with salt, pepper and the poultry seasoning.
- Fold in the oysters.
- If the dressing is too dry add some of the oyster liquor.

Gravy

Giblet broth
¼ cup flour

Giblets and neck meat

- Using the roasting pan, heat the drippings from the turkey.
- Stir in the flour.
- Slowly pour the broth from the turkey giblet and neck pan into the roasting pan until the gravy is thickened. Stir in the chopped liver, heart and meat from the neck
- Serve the gravy in a gravy boat or pitcher. For a richer gravy, add cream until thickened in place of the broth.
- Serve the turkey with cranberry chutney or cranberry relish.

TURKEY HASH

Serves 4

3 cups leftover turkey
1 cup onion, chopped
2 cups potatoes, cubed

½ stick butter
Salt and pepper
½ teaspoon rosemary

- In a skillet saute the potatoes and onions in the butter until tender. Add the rosemary, turkey, salt and pepper.
- Serve hot with ketchup.

ROAST GOOSE

Serves 6

8 pound goose
1 apple, cored and sliced

1 onion, sliced
Coarse salt

- ♦ Heat the oven to 350°.
- ♦ Rinse the goose. Rub the skin with the salt.
- ♦ Place the apples and onion in the cavity.
- ♦ Put the goose in a roasting pan and bake 20 minutes to pound, until crisp on outside.

Cumberland Sauce

¼ cup red currant jelly
1 tablespoon Madeira
1 tablespoon Sherry
2 tablespoons orange juice
1 tablespoon lemon juice

½ teaspoon dry mustard
½ teaspoon paprika
½ teaspoon ground ginger
1 Tbls. orange peel, grated

- ♦ Heat the jelly until it melts.
- ♦ Add Madeira, Sherry, juices and spices.
- ♦ Serve at room temperature.

Mushroom Sauce

¼ cup butter
½ pound mushrooms
1 clove garlic, crushed

2 tablespoons flour
1 cup chicken broth
¼ cup Sherry

- ♦ In a saucepan heat 2 tablespoons of butter.
- ♦ Saute the mushrooms and garlic. Remove the mushrooms.
- ♦ Melt the rest of the butter. Stir in the flour and gradually add the chicken broth.
- ♦ Add wine and bring to a boil. Add the mushrooms.

MEAT AND GAME

Barn – Eastern Shore of Maryland

A number of different animals are raised in the Chesapeake Bay region for their meat. This includes pork, beef, and lamb. In addition venison is readily available during the deer hunting season, and rabbit. In earlier times, squirrel and muskrat were even popular, and were used in Brunswick Stew in lieu of chicken.

VENISON STEW IN RED WINE

Serves 6

2 pounds venison
¼ cup flour
½ stick butter
1 large onion, chopped
2 cloves garlic, minced

½ cup red wine
1 cup beef broth
½ jar currant jelly
Salt and pepper to taste

- ◆ Cut the venison into cubes and roll in flour.
- ◆ In a skillet, brown the onion and garlic in the butter. Remove and add the venison and brown. Add red wine and beef broth. Stir well. Simmer for 2-3 hours until meat is tender, adding more wine or broth, to keep from drying out.
- ◆ Season with salt and pepper and add currant jam.
- ◆ Serve with noodles or rice.

VENISON STEW

2 pounds cubed venison
2 tablespoons butter
1 medium onion, chopped
1 green pepper, chopped
6 potatoes, chopped

1 tablespoon parsley
1½ cups water
1 teaspoon salt
1 teaspoon pepper

- ◆ In a heavy pan or Dutch oven braise the venison in the butter.
- ◆ Add the other ingredients. Simmer for 2-3 hours, until the meat is tender.
- ◆ Serve with rice or noodles.

VENISON BURGERS

Makes 8 burgers

2 pounds ground venison
2 tablespoons horseradish
¼ cup ketchup

2 tablespoons Worcestershire
Salt and pepper

- Combine all the ingredients and make into patties.
- Cook on grill until desired doneness.
- Serve on rolls.

STUFFED COUNTRY HAM

12 pound country ham
2 pounds spinach
¼ cup butter
1 pound watercress
2 stalks celery

1 tsp. crushed red pepper
1 teaspoon black pepper
1 teaspoon salt
½ pound mustard greens
¼ cup green onions

- Place the ham in a large pot and cover with water. Let sit overnight.
- Replace the water and cook the ham until the water boils, then simmer for one hour. Take the ham out of the pot and place on a cutting board. Cut the rind off the ham.
- Chop the spinach, watercress, celery, mustard greens and green onions.
- Melt the butter in a large saucepan. Add the green onions and celery, and cook for 5 minutes.
- Add the other green vegetables, and cook for 15 minutes over low heat.
- Cut six incisions in the ham and stuff with the vegetables.
- Cover the ham with cheesecloth and tie with a string.
- Return the ham to the cooking pot and cook 15 minutes to the pound.
- Remove the ham from the pot.
- Leaving the cheesecloth on, place the ham on a platter and let sit overnight in the refrigerator.
- Before serving remove the cheesecloth and slice the ham in thin slices.

STUFFED HAM ENCROUTE

5 pound ham, boneless and cooked
2 pounds mushrooms, sliced
½ stick butter
1 onion, chopped

¼ cup sherry
1 cup liver pate
½ teaspoon sage or thyme
Allspice, to taste
Salt and pepper, to taste

♦ Saute the mushrooms in the butter and add the chopped onions until tender. Add the sherry, salt and pepper to taste. Blend in the rest of the ingredients, except ham.

Pastry

1¼ cups flour

1 stick butter
¼ cup water

♦ In a food processor blend all the ingredients until a ball is formed.
♦ Roll out in a circle the size of the ham.
♦ Spread the dough with the pate and place the ham in the center.
♦ Roll up the dough so ham is completely covered and seal the edges. Bake at 375° for 45 minutes until the crust is golden.

PORK TENDERLOIN

Serves 8

4 pounds pork tenderloin.

Dry Rub

¼ cup cracked pepper
2 Tbls. coarse salt
2 Tbls. garlic powder
¼ cup brown sugar

1 teaspoon celery salt
1 teaspoon cayenne
1 tablespoon rosemary

♦ Combine the dry rub ingredients in a bowl.
♦ Place the pork on a platter and rub the dry rub into the meat on both sides.
♦ Grill on a charcoal or gas grill until desired doneness.

VIRGINIA HAM

Virginia hams are world famous. The most noted is the Smithfield Ham Company. Smithfield hams were first shipped to England in 1639. The company uses a special curing process, and then the hams are smoked and aged. Smithfield hams come from hogs that are fed peanuts, another southern staple. Country hams are similar, but do not necessarily come from peanut-fed hogs. The hams are served thinly sliced, used in soups, sandwiches, with biscuits, and a variety of other uses.

APPLES AND PORK

Serves 6

6 good size pork chops
3 apples, cored and sliced
1 small onion, sliced

¼ cup butter
¼ cup bourbon or rum
1 teaspoon cinnamon

- ◆ Preheat the oven to 350°.
- ◆ Brown the pork chops in ½ of butter in an iron skillet.
- ◆ Remove the chops from the skillet. Add the rest of butter and saute apples and onion in the skillet.
- ◆ Place the pork chops over the apples.
- ◆ Pour bourbon and cinnamon over chops.
- ◆ Bake in the oven for 45 minutes.
- ◆ This is also good substituting ½ cup cider for the rum.

CRANBERRY PORK CHOPS

Serves 4

4 thick pork chops
½ cup bread crumbs

1 tablespoon rosemary
½ cup cranberry chutney

- ◆ Cut a pocket in the pork chops.
- ◆ Combine the chutney and bread crumbs.
- ◆ Stuff the pork chop pockets with the bread mixture. Sprinkle the pork chops with rosemary.
- ◆ Bake at 350° for 45 minutes.
- ◆ Serve on a platter with extra chutney.

SAUSAGE SPAGHETTI

Serves 4

1 pound Italian mild sausage
1 15 ounce can diced tomatoes
2 tablespoons olive oil
2 cloves garlic, crushed
1 tablespoon oregano

¼ teaspoon cayenne
½ teaspoon chili powder
1 small onion, chopped
½ pound cooked spaghetti
1 cup fresh parmesan cheese

♦ Brown the sausages in a skillet. Remove and cut into 1" pieces.
♦ In a saucepan saute the onion in the olive oil until transparent.
♦ Add the garlic, oregano, cayenne and chili powder.
♦ Place the spaghetti in a large bowl, cover with sausage and pour sauce over the top. Serve with freshly grated parmesan cheese.

SHISH-KEBAB

Serves 6-8

3 pounds lamb
2 large tomatoes
2 large onions
4 large cloves garlic, crushed
½ cup olive oil

1 green pepper
1 red pepper
½ pound mushrooms
2 tablespoons fresh rosemary

♦ Combine the cloves, olive oil and rosemary in a large bowl.
♦ Cut the lamb into 1 inch cubes and pieces in a bowl. Cover with the marinade. Refrigerate at least one hour before cooking.
♦ Cut the vegetables into bite size pieces.
♦ On skewers alternate vegetables and lamb pieces.
♦ Cook on grill until meat is desired doneness.

Sauce

1 cup sour cream
12 large mint leaves

Juice of ½ lemon

♦ Combine the ingredients in a bowl. Refrigerate and serve with shish-kebabs.

Gazpacho
Grilled Leg of Lamb
Roasted Potatoes
Salad
Cheese Herb Bread
Key Lime Pie

GRILLED LEG OF LAMB

Serve 8

4 pounds boneless leg of lamb

Dry Rub

¼ cup cracked pepper	1 teaspoon celery salt
2 Tbls. coarse salt	1 teaspoon cayenne
2 Tbls. garlic powder	¼ cup fresh rosemary

◆ Combine the dry rub ingredients in a bowl.
◆ Place the lamb on a platter and rub the dry rub into the meat on both sides.
◆ Grill on a charcoal or gas grill until desired doneness.
◆ Serve with mint sauce or horseradish sauce.

Mint Sauce

1 cup white wine vinegar	½ cup fresh mint

◆ Combine the vinegar and mint in a jar. Store until ready to serve.

Rosemary Marinade

This can be used in place of the dry rub.

¼ cup olive oil	¼ cup rosemary
¼ cup lemon juice	2 cloves garlic, crushed

◆ Combine all the ingredients in a bowl. Marinate the lamb overnight.

Around the Fire

Oysters and Bacon Appetizer
Lamb Pie
Green Salad
Apple Brown Betty

LAMB PIE

Serves 6

♦ This hearty winter's dish can be made from leftover lamb. Venison can be substituted for the lamb.

Filling:

1 cup celery, diced	¼ cup butter
1 cup carrots, diced	3 cups leftover lamb
½ cup onion, chopped	½ cup flour
¼ cup green or red pepper, diced	2 cups beef broth

♦ Saute the vegetables in butter until crisp, but slightly tender.
♦ Cut the lamb into 1 inch cubes and add to the vegetables.
♦ Stir in the flour and slowly add the beef broth. Stir until thickened.
♦ Place this mixture in a 2 quart glass baking dish.

Crust:

6 tablespoons butter	1 ½ teaspoons baking powder
2 cups flour	½ cup grated cheddar cheese
¾ cup half and half	

♦ Place all the ingredients in a food processor. Blend until a ball is formed.
♦ On a floured cutting board roll out the dough to fit the shape of the baking dish.
♦ Lay the dough over the top of the lamb mixture.
♦ Bake at 350° for 45 minutes, or until the crust is browned.

LAMB PATTIES

Serves 4-6

2 pounds ground lamb
4 cloves garlic, crushed
2 Tbls. fresh ginger, grated

1 teaspoon cumin
¼ cup raisins
½ cup water

- Boil the raisins in the saucepan with the water until softened. Drain.
- In a bowl combine together the lamb, garlic, ginger, cumin and raisins.
- Shape into patties.
- Grill on a barbecue, under the broiler, or on a stovetop grill.
- Serve on rolls with Dijon mustard.

STEAK WITH BORDELAISE SAUCE

Serves 8

4 pounds sirloin

Dry Rub

¼ cup cracked pepper
2 Tbls. coarse salt
2 teaspoons garlic powder

1 teaspoon celery salt
1 teaspoon cayenne

- Combine the dry rub ingredients in a bowl.
- Place the beef on platter and rub the dry rub into the meat on both sides.
- Grill on a charcoal or gas grill until desired doneness.

Bordelaise Sauce

2 tablespoons butter
2 tablespoons shallots, minced
1½ cups beef broth

2 tablespoons lemon juice
2 tablespoons parsley, chopped
½ cup mushrooms

- Melt the butter in a saucepan and add shallots.
- Add the wine, and then other ingredients, until reduced by one-half.
- Serve in a pitcher with the steak.

BEEF TENDERLOIN CHEZ CONDUIT

Serve this beef dish for an elegant seated dinner or as a hors d'oeuvre. The combination of the Bearnaise sauce and spices of the dry rub make this an easy, but oh so good entrée.

Serves 8

4 pounds beef tenderloin

Dry Rub

¼ cup cracked pepper   1 teaspoon celery salt
2 Tbls. coarse salt   1 teaspoon cayenne
2 Tabls. garlic powder

- ◆ Combine the dry rub ingredients in a bowl.
- ◆ Place the beef on platter and rub the dry rub into the meat on both sides.
- ◆ Grill on a charcoal or gas grill until desired doneness.

Bearnaise Sauce

2 Tbls. white wine vinegar   1 stick butter
2 tablespoons white wine   3 egg yolks
1 tablespoon chopped shallots   ½ lemon
1 tablespoon fresh tarragon   Salt and pepper

- ◆ Melt the butter and pour into a food processor. Add egg yolks and lemon juice.
- ◆ Combine the vinegar, white wine, shallots and tarragon in a small saucepan. Bring to a boil and reduce to about half.
- ◆ Add to food processor mixture. Season with salt and pepper.
- ◆ Serve the sauce in a bowl with the tenderloin.

SHEPHERD'S PIE

Shepherd's pie can made from many leftover meats and mashed potatoes. Our favorites are lamb or beef. 1 pound cooked hamburger can also be used.

Serves 6

3 cups leftover cooked meat
2 cups beef bouillon
½ cup flour
2 Tbls. Worcestershire sauce

1 tablespoon butter
¼ cup onion, chopped
3 cups mashed potatoes
Parmesan cheese

- Preheat the oven to 350°.
- In a skillet saute the onion in the butter. Add flour and slowly stir in the hot beef bouillon.
- When thickened add cooked meat and Worcestershire sauce.
- Place meat mixture in a baking dish.
- Cover with mashed potatoes. Sprinkle with Parmesan cheese.
- Bake in oven for 30 minutes, until the cheese is slightly browned.

BLUE CHEESE BURGERS

Makes 6 burgers

2 pounds ground beef
½ pound blue cheese
¼ cup chopped onions

1 teaspoon garlic salt
Pepper

- Combine the ground beef with onions, garlic salt and pepper.
- Shape into round patties. Place the patties on a platter and make hole in each burger.
- Stuff the burgers with a large tablespoon of blue cheese and then seal meat.
- Cook on a grill until done.
- This is delicious on a hot summer night, served on rolls with salad and homemade French fries.

SPAGHETTI

Serves 4

1 pound ground beef
1 15 ounce can diced tomatoes
1 small onion, chopped
2 cloves garlic
1 tablespoon olive oil
1 tablespoon oregano

1 teaspoon sugar
¼ teaspoon cayenne
½ pound spaghetti
1 cup grated parmesan cheese

- ◆ Cook the ground beef and onion in skillet.
- ◆ In a saucepan heat the olive oil and add onion, cooking till transparent.
- ◆ Stir in the garlic tomato sauce, oregano, sugar and cayenne. Pour over the meat mixture.
- ◆ In large pot of boiling water cook spaghetti until tender, about 9-10 minutes.
- ◆ Serve the spaghetti with the meat sauce on top on individual plates. Sprinkle with Parmesan cheese.

KAY'S LASAGNA

Serves 6

1 pound ground beef
1 15 ounce can tomato sauce
1 small onion, chopped
2 cloves garlic, minced
1 teaspoon oregano

3 scallions, chopped
8 ounces cream cheese
1 cup sour cream
1 pound noodles

- ◆ Brown the beef and onions in a skillet.
- ◆ Add the tomato sauce, garlic and oregano.
- ◆ In a bowl combine the scallions, sour cream and cream cheese.
- ◆ Cook the noodles according to the directions.
- ◆ In casserole put in a layer of noodles, then sour cream mix and top with beef. Repeat.
- ◆ Bake 35 minutes at 350°.

PIZZA

Dough

1 cup lukewarm water
1 package yeast
3 ½ cups flour

1 teaspoon olive oil
½ teaspoon salt

- Dissolve the yeast in the water.
- In a food processor combine the flour and olive oil. Slowly add yeast water.
- On a floured board roll out the dough into the size of a cookie sheet. Place on oiled cookie sheet.

Sauce

1 15 ounce can tomato sauce
2 cloves garlic, crushed
1 small onion, chopped

1 tablespoon oregano
1 tablespoon olive oil

- Heat the oven to 500°.
- In a saucepan saute the onion in olive oil. Then add tomato sauce, garlic and oregano.
- Pour the sauce over the dough leaving one inch on all sides.

1 pound cooked sausage or pepperoni, sliced

2 cups mozzarella cheese, grated

- Sprinkle the sausage and then cheese over the tomato sauce.
- Turn oven down to 425° and bake pizza 15 to 20 minutes, until the filling is bubbly and the crust browned. Serve immediately.

PIZZA VARIATIONS

Using the above recipe for pizza you can substitute these items:
- 1 pound crab meat for sausage and 2 cups grated Gruyere or Jarlsberg cheese
- 1 pound cooked ground beef and 2 cups Monterey Jack cheese
- Vegetarian – substitute ½ cup broccoli, ½ cup carrots, ¼ cup green pepper, ¼ cup red pepper, 2 tablespoons fresh basil and 2 cups Monterey Jack cheese.

CHILI

Serves 4

1 pound ground beef	2 tablespoons chili powder
1 15 ounce can tomato sauce	2 large cloves garlic, crushed
1 15 ounce can kidney beans	2 green chiles, chopped
1 small onion, chopped	¼ teaspoon cayenne

♦ Brown the beef in a skillet with a little olive oil and add onions. Add the other ingredients.

Tacos

Taco Shells	Sour cream
Lettuce, shredded	Refried beans, heated
Chopped tomato	Black olives, sliced
Monterey Jack cheese	

♦ In each taco shell place some of the chili and top with any of the above ingredients.

LILI'S BEEF BURGANDY

This recipe can use any type of beef, including chuck as the long cooking time and wine tenderize the meat.

3 pounds cubed beef	½ cup Burgandy wine
1 envelop dry onion soup mix	2 cans cream of mushroom soup

♦ Preheat the oven to 250°.
♦ Combine all the ingredients in a large casserole.
♦ Cover with tin foil.
♦ Bake for 5 hours.
♦ Serve over rice or noodles.

STUFFED ZUCCHINI

Serves 8

4 large zucchini
1 medium onion, chopped
2 tablespoons butter
2 cloves garlic, mashed
1½ cups mushrooms, chopped
2 pounds ground beef or lamb

¼ cup parmesan cheese
Salt and pepper to taste
1 egg
¼ cup bread crumbs
Olive oil
Tomato sauce

- Parboil the whole zucchini, drain and cut in half lengthwise. Remove some of the pulp from the center and save.
- Melt the butter in a saucepan and saute the onion and mushrooms. Add the garlic, chopped beef, parmesan cheese, salt, pepper, and the pulp from the zucchini.
- Stir in the egg and mix well.
- Place the zucchini shells in a buttered baking dish.
- Fill with the meat mixture.
- Sprinkle with bread crumbs and dribble the olive oil over the crumbs.
- Bake at 375° for 30 minutes, until browned.
- Serve with extra tomato sauce.
- Eggplant can be substituted for zucchini.

STUFFED PEPPERS

Serves 6

6 green peppers
1 pound ground beef
2 cups cooked rice
1 15 ounce can tomato sauce

1 teaspoon oregano
2 cloves garlic, crushed
1 small onion, chopped
Salt and pepper

- Cut tops off the green peppers, removing the seeds, but saving extra green pepper.
- Brown the ground beef and onion in a skillet. Add ½ can of the tomato sauce, chopped green pepper from top, and rice. Season with salt and pepper.
- Stuff the peppers with the mixture. Bake 20 minutes at 350°.
- In sauce pan heat the rest of the tomato sauce and oregano.
- Pour the sauce over the peppers.

CASSOULET

Cassoulet is a hearty French dish that uses game, pork and beans. This recipe takes quite a while to prepare and will serve 20 or more people. You may have to use several casseroles. A large roasting pan will also work.

3 ½ pounds navy beans
2 bay leaves
½ teaspoon thyme
¼ cup parsley
1½ pounds pork skin (cut in strips)
4 pound shoulder pork, without skin
1 pork hock

½ pound bacon
4 cloves garlic, crushed
5 pound goose
1 onion, stuck with two cloves of garlic
Salt and pepper
2 pounds pork sausage
¾ cup goose fat

- Cut the goose into quarters and remove the fat. Rub the goose with salt and refrigerate in a large pot overnight.
- Take the goose out of the pot and rub the salt off. Rinse out the pot. Add ½ goose fat, ¼ teaspoon thyme and 1 bay leaf.
- Put the goose back in the pot. Cook for 30 minutes. Prick the goose. If the juices are clear the goose is done. Save the fat.
- Soak the beans in water for 4 hours. Drain the water.
- In a large pot combine 2 quarts water, ¼ teaspoon thyme, 1 bay leaf, the pork hock, the pork skins, onion, salt and pepper. Cover and cook until the beans are tender.
- Fry the sausage in the rest of the goose fat for 10 minutes.
- Cut the pork shoulder into 2 inch cubes and brown in the fat from the sausage.
- Place the pork in a saucepan with the garlic and bacon. Add 4 cups of water and cook until the pork is tender.
- In a bowl pour in the liquid from the beans and pork and set aside.
- In a large earthenware casserole put a layer of beans, a layer of the pork, bacon rinds and sausage.
- Add another layer of the beans and top with the goose.
- Pour the liquid mixture over the casserole.
- Cover and bake for 1½ hours in a 350° oven.

KAY'S CHILI MACARONI

Long before Southwestern cooking became popular in the United States, my mother would fix this easy, but good dish.

Serves 4

1 large onion, chopped	2 cups water
1 tablespoon olive oil	1 tablespoon sugar
1 pound sweet sausage	½ teaspoon salt
1 large can tomatoes	Pepper
2 cups elbow macaroni	1 tablespoon chili powder

- ◆ Brown the onion in the olive oil in a skillet.
- ◆ Add the sausage and brown.
- ◆ Add other ingredients and cook until macaroni is tender.
- ◆ Serve as a main course.

HARMONY HILLS' TONGUE

Harmony Hills was the name of my maternal grandparents' farm in Havre de Grace. One dish my grandmother's cook loved to fix was tongue, something that is no longer on most menus, but is absolutely delicious.

4 pound fresh tongue	½ cup vinegar
4 cups water	¾ cup raisins
2 small onions, finely chopped	½ teaspoon ginger
¾ cup brown sugar	1 cup crumbled ginger snaps

- ◆ Preheat the oven to 300°.
- ◆ Place the tongue with water in a baking dish and cook for four hours in the oven.
- ◆ Remove the tongue and save the water.
- ◆ In the pan mix the water, onions, brown sugar, vinegar and raisins. Simmer to ½ liquid.
- ◆ Add the ginger snaps.
- ◆ Serve the sauce hot with the sliced tongue.

LIVER AND ONIONS

Serves 4

2 pounds calf's liver
1 cup onions, sliced
½ stick butter
1 Tbls. parsley, chopped

1 teaspoon marjoram
1 teaspoon basil
½ teaspoon sage

- Saute the onions in ½ the butter in a skillet.
- Remove the onions and saute the liver in the rest of the butter.
- Add the herbs.
- Cover the liver with the onions.
- Serve immediately. Garnish with parsley.

KIDNEY STEW

When I was growing up, I was the only child in my family who liked kidney stew. Today it's not served very often, and it's very high in cholesterol.

Serves 4

2 beef kidneys
1 cup water
½ cup red wine vinegar
Salt and pepper
¼ cup flour
¼ cup butter

¼ cup olive oil
2 cloves garlic, crushed
1 cup onion, chopped
1 teaspoon rosemary
1 cup red wine
1 cup beef broth

- Place the kidneys in a bowl and cover with water and the vinegar. Let stand two hours. Drain.
- Cut the kidneys into slices and sprinkle with the salt and pepper. Dredge in the flour.
- In a skillet heat the butter and olive oil, and brown the kidneys.
- Add garlic, onion, and rosemary. Cook five minutes.
- Add the wine and beef broth. Simmer 15 minutes.
- Serve with noodles.

VEGETABLES

Marsh – Eastern Shore of Maryland

Chesapeake Bay vegetables are at their peak during the summer months. Corn, tomatoes, peas, beans, lettuce, cucumbers, onions, peppers, and squash are among the many varieties available.

GREEN BEANS

Serves 8

2 ½ pounds green beans
¼ cup olive oil

1 Tbls. grated lemon rind
½ teaspoon red pepper flakes

- Cook the beans in a large pot of boiling water for 6 minutes.
- Drain the beans and add the olive oil, lemon rind and red pepper.
- This dish may be served hot or cold.
- Marinating this overnight in the refrigerator adds flavor to the beans.

LEMONY GREEN BEANS

Serves 8

2 ½ pounds green beans
Juice of ½ lemon
Grated rind from lemon

1 jar sliced pimento
¼ cup olive oil

- Cook the beans in a pan of boiling water for 6 minutes. Drain the water.
- Squeeze the lemon juice over the beans and add the olive oil and lemon rind.
- Wrap a pimento strip around six beans, and continue until all are wrapped.
- Place on a serving tray.
- This is a very colorful dish at Christmas.

GREEN BEAN CASSEROLE

Serves 6-8

2 pounds green beans
1 can cream of mushroom soup

Salt and pepper
1 can French fried onions

- Cook the beans until just tender. Place in a casserole dish.
- Pour the soup over the beans and cover with the onions.
- Bake 350° for 25 minutes.

CORN FRITTERS

Serves 6

2 cups fresh corn
2 eggs, separated
½ cup flour
1 teaspoon baking powder

½ teaspoon salt
1 Tbls. green chiles, chopped
Butter

- In a bowl mix the corn with the egg yolks.
- Add the flour, baking powder, salt and chiles.
- Beat the egg whites until peaks are formed.
- Fold into the corn mixture.
- Drop by spoonful into a hot skillet with butter and brown.
- Serve hot or cold. If served cold this is a delicious appetizer with salsa.

EASY, BUT DELICIOUS CORN ON THE COB

Serves 6

6-12 ears of corn

- In an electric skillet heat water to cover corn. Boil corn for 7 minutes.
- Remove and serve immediately with butter.

111

SUCCOTASH

Serves 4-6

2 cups fresh lima beans
2 cups fresh corn

¼ cup butter
Salt and pepper, to taste

- Put the lima beans in a saucepan and add just enough water to cover. Bring to a boil, cover and simmer for 15 minutes.
- Add the corn and simmer for 10 more minutes.
- Drain the water, season with salt and pepper.
- Dill may also be added for additional flavor.

LIMA BEANS

Serves 6

3 cups shelled lima beans
¼ cup fresh dill, chopped

½ stick butter

- Cook the lima beans in boiling water until tender. Drain.
- Add dill and butter.

SPINACH PIE

1 9" pie crust
1 cup shredded Swiss cheese
¼ cups parmesan cheese
1¼ cups milk

1 package fresh spinach
¼ cup chopped onion
4 eggs
1 Tbls. Worcestershire sauce

- Cook spinach in just a little boiling water until just tender.
- Layer the spinach, onion and cheeses in the pie crust.
- Beat together the milk, eggs and Worcestershire sauce.
- Pour over the spinach mixture.
- Bake for 10 minutes at 450°, then reduce oven to 325° and bake for another 25 minutes.
- Serve hot or cold.

CREAMED SPINACH

Serves 6-8

2 pounds fresh spinach
8 ounces cream cheese
1 stick butter, melted

¼ teaspoon nutmeg
Salt and pepper to taste

- ◆ Heat the oven to 350°.
- ◆ Wash the spinach and take off steams.
- ◆ Combine all the ingredients and put in a baking dish.
- ◆ Bake for 30 minutes.

SPINACH SOUFFLE

Broccoli can be substituted for the spinach.

Serves 4

1 box frozen spinach or
1 pound fresh cooked spinach
1 cup half and half
½ stick butter

¼ cup flour
½ cup sharp cheddar cheese
4 eggs, separated

- ◆ Drain the spinach in a colander.
- ◆ In medium sized saucepan melt the butter.
- ◆ Stir in the flour and slowly add the half and half until thickened.
- ◆ Stir in the egg yolks, cheese and add the spinach.
- ◆ Beat the egg whites until stiff and fold into the spinach mixture.
- ◆ Pour into a souffle dish.
- ◆ Bake at 350° for 45 minutes.

ELIZABETH LAY'S BROCCOLI CASSEROLE

Serves 4

2 cups broccoli florets
1 can water chestnuts, sliced
1 cup mayonnaise

1 cup grated cheddar cheese
1 can cream of chicken soup
½ cup fresh bread crumbs

- ♦ Preheat the oven to 350°.
- ♦ Combine all the ingredients, except bread crumbs, and place in a baking dish.
- ♦ Cover with bread crumbs.
- ♦ Bake 20 minutes or until bubbly.

Now Let Us Praise Fried Pies

EASY BROCCOLI

Serves 6

2 pounds fresh broccoli

1 lemon

- ♦ Cook the broccoli until just tender.
- ♦ Place in a serving dish. Squeeze the lemon over the broccoli.
- ♦ This can be served hot or cold.

SUMMER EGGPLANT

Serves 4-6

1 large eggplant
½ cup flour
½ teaspoon salt

2 tablespoons olive oil
2 tablespoons butter

- ♦ Combine the flour and salt in a bowl.
- ♦ Cut the eggplant into ¼ inch slices. Dip in the flour and salt mix.
- ♦ Fry the eggplant in butter and olive oil until browned on each side.
- ♦ This can be served plain or with tomato sauce.

ZUCCHINI TART

Pastry

1¼ cups flour
¼ pound butter
1 teaspoon salt

1 teaspoon sugar
¼ cup ice water

- ♦ Combine the flour, salt, butter and sugar in a food processor.
- ♦ With the machine running add the water. When a ball is formed stop the machine.
- ♦ Roll the pastry out on a lightly floured board into a large circle to fit a 10 inch porcelain quiche pan.

Filling

2 tablespoons Dijon mustard
3 cups zucchini, grated
2 cups grated Monterey Jack cheese
8 ounces cream cheese

1 cup heavy cream
2 eggs
Salt and pepper to taste
4 green chiles, seeded and diced

- ♦ Preheat the oven to 450°.
- ♦ With a dull knife spread the mustard on the pastry shell and bake for ten minutes.
- ♦ Remove the shell from the oven.
- ♦ Reduce the oven temperature to 350°.
- ♦ When the shell is cooled sprinkle one-half of the Monterey Jack cheese over the pastry.
- ♦ Put the grated zucchini in a colander, sprinkle with salt and let drain.
- ♦ Spread the zucchini and green chiles over the Monterey Jack cheese.
- ♦ In a mixing bowl beat together the cream cheese, eggs, salt and pepper. Pour over the zucchini.
- ♦ Sprinkle the remaining cheese on top.
- ♦ Bake for 45 minutes, or until set.

ZUCCHINI CASSEROLE

Serves 8

2 large zucchini
4 tomatoes

1 teaspoon fresh oregano
½ cup parmesan cheese

- Boil the tomatoes for 5 minutes. Score the bottom to make for easier peeling. Peel the skins and mash tomatoes
- Add the oregano.
- Cut the zucchini into thin slices and put into a baking dish.
- Top with tomato mixture.
- Then sprinkle with parmesan cheese.
- Bake at 350° for 30 minutes, or until slightly browned.

CHEESY POTATOES

Serves 8

8 large baking potatoes
½ stick butter
½ -1 cup half and half

Salt and pepper, to taste
4 cloves garlic, minced
½ pound cheddar cheese

- Place the potatoes in a 350° oven for one hour. (They can also be done in a microwave, cooked until tender).
- Remove just the very top of each potato and scoop out pulp.
- Place the potato pulp in a bowl.
- Add butter, salt and pepper. Start out with ½ cup half and half. Add more if the mashed potato mixture is too thick.
- Add cheese. Beat well.
- Stuff the potato skins with the potato mixture.
- Place under a broiler until heated.
- Serve immediately.
- To vary the taste, add grated garlic or chives to the mashed potatoes.
- Cooked broccoli or bacon is also good.

POTATO FRITTATA

½ pound red bliss potatoes
1 onion, chopped
1 teaspoon fresh rosemary
4 eggs

¼ cup half and half
Salt and pepper
¼ cup grated parmesan cheese
Olive oil

- ◆ Cook the potatoes in a pot of boiling water until tender.
- ◆ Saute the onion and rosemary in olive oil in a skillet.
- ◆ Add the potatoes to the skillet, and mash the potatoes with a fork.
- ◆ In a bowl beat the eggs, half and half, salt and pepper to taste.
- ◆ Add the parmesan cheese.
- ◆ Pour the egg mixture over potatoes. Just mix slightly.
- ◆ Allow to cook for about ten minutes, or until set.
- ◆ Remove from the heat and serve for brunch, as a side dish or hors d'oeuvres, cut into squares.

GARLIC MASHED POTATOES

Serves 8 or more

12 large red potatoes
½ stick butter
2 large cloves garlic, crushed

½ -1 cup half and half
Salt and pepper to taste

- ◆ In a large pan boil the potatoes with the skins on, until tender, about ½ hour.
- ◆ Drain the water and put the potatoes in a large bowl.
- ◆ Add butter, half and half, garlic, salt and pepper and beat together. Use more half and half if too stiff. Do not overmix.
- ◆ Serve immediately.

ROASTED POTATOES

Serves 6

9 red or 6 sweet potatoes
2 onions
¼ cup olive oil

1 tablespoon rosemary
1 tablespoon coarse salt

♦ Preheat the oven to 375°.
♦ In an iron skillet put ½ of the olive oil.
♦ Cut the potatoes and onions into bite size pieces.
♦ Place in a baking dish or iron skillet.
♦ Sprinkle with rosemary, salt and rest of olive oil.
♦ Bake in oven for 45 minutes, tossing mixture every 15 minutes. Cook until the potatoes are tender.

PARBOILED ROASTED POTATOES

Serves six

9 red potatoes
2 onions, cubed
¼ cup olive oil

1 tablespoon rosemary
1 tablespoon coarse salt

♦ Cut potatoes into large cubes, leaving skins on. Parboil until just tender.
♦ In a large bowl put the potatoes, onions, rosemary, olive oil and salt. Combine with a large spoon.
♦ This can either be baked in the oven as in Roasted Potatoes, though only bake for ½ hour
♦ Or put on a grill and roast till browned.

DILLY POTATOES AND PEAS

This is a perfect dish with salmon on the Fourth of July.

Serves 6

2 cups fresh peas
6 large red potatoes

¼ cup fresh chopped dill
¼ cup melted butter

- In a pan of boiling water cook the potatoes until tender, about 25 minutes.
- Add peas and cook 5 minutes more. Drain the water.
- Add the dill and butter.
- Serve immediately in a serving dish.

POTATOES AU GRATIN

Serves 4

4 large baking potatoes
¼ cup butter
1 teaspoon salt
½ tsp. Worcestershire sauce
Pepper

1 cup Gruyere cheese, grated
2 Tbls. fresh parsley, chopped
¼ cup onion, chopped
½ cup half and half

- Preheat the oven to 350°.
- Peel and cut the potatoes into ¼ inch slices and place in a 9" x 13" baking dish. Dot with butter, and sprinkle on remaining ingredients.
- Pour the cream over the potatoes.
- Cover with tin foil and bake for one hour.

PARSLEY RED POTATOES

Serves 6-8

8 large red potatoes
¼ cup melted butter

¼ cup fresh parsley, chopped
Salt and pepper, to taste

- In a large pot, boil the potatoes until tender. Drain
- Place the potatoes in a serving bowl and pour the butter over the top.
- Sprinkle parsley, salt and pepper on the potatoes. Serve immediately.

CANDIED SWEET POTATOES

Serves 6

6 large sweet potatoes
½ stick butter
½ cup milk

¼ cup brown sugar
½ cup pecans

- Preheat oven to 350°.
- Bake potatoes in the oven for one hour or until tender.
- Remove from the oven and peel the skins off.
- Combine the potatoes in a bowl with butter, milk, and brown sugar and beat together. Add pecans.
- Pour into a casserole and bake at 350° for ½ hour.
- Children prefer to substitute miniature marshmallows for the pecans. These should be placed on top of the casserole before baking.

PEARLIE-MAMA'S SWEET POTATO SOUFFLE

This can be served as a vegetable dish or dessert. It is quite sweet.

3 cup mashed sweet potatoes
2 eggs, beaten
½ cup milk
1 cup sugar

½ teaspoon salt
1/3 stick butter
1 teaspoon vanilla

- Preheat the oven to 350°.
- Combine the ingredients and pour into a baking dish.

Topping

1 stick melted butter
1 cup brown sugar
1/3 cup flour

1 cup chopped nuts
1 teaspoon cinnamon

- In a saucepan melt the butter. Add the sugar, flour, cinnamon and nuts. Crumble topping over souffle. Bake for 35 minutes.

Now Let Us Praise Fried Pies

SHERRIED SWEET POTATOES

Serves 6

6 large sweet potatoes
½ cup brown sugar
1 cup orange juice
¼ cup raisins

¼ cup sherry
¼ cup pecans, toasted
1 tsp. shredded orange peel

- ◆ Peel the sweet potatoes and cook in boiling water until tender.
- ◆ Mash the potatoes in a bowl and add the rest of the ingredients.
- ◆ Pour into a casserole and bake for 30 minutes at 350°.

ASPARAGUS CASSEROLE

Serves 4

20 stalks asparagus
½ stick butter
¼ cup flour
1 cup milk

1 cup cheddar cheese, grated
Salt and pepper to taste
½ cup almonds

- ◆ Melt the butter in a saucepan.
- ◆ Add flour and slowly stir in milk until thickened.
- ◆ Stir in the grated cheese. More milk can be added if too thick.
- ◆ Place the asparagus in a casserole dish and pour the sauce over them. Sprinkle the grated cheese and almonds on top.
- ◆ Bake at 350° for 20 minutes.

SESAME ASPARAGUS

This dish can be served hot or cold

Serves 4

1 pound asparagus   1 lemon
2 tablespoons sesame seeds

- ◆ Boil water in an electric frying pan or skillet.
- ◆ Place the asparagus in boiling water, covered, for seven minutes. Remove and put on a flat serving dish. Sprinkle with sesame seeds and juice of the lemon.

MINTED CARROTS

Serves 4-6

8 medium carrots, peeled, cut   ¼ cup mint, chopped
lengthwise in half, and sliced   Mint leaves
¼ cup butter

- ◆ In a skillet saute the carrots in butter until tender. Add the chopped mint.
- ◆ Place on a serving dish and decorate with mint leaves.

CANDIED CARROTS

Serves 8

1 pound carrots   ½ cup butter
½ cup brown sugar

- ◆ Peel and slice the carrots lengthwise cutting in half.
- ◆ In a skillet melt the butter and add sugar.
- ◆ Add the carrots and cook until tender.

LILI'S CARROTS GRAND MARNIER

Serves 6-8 as a side dish.

1 pound carrots, peeled and
sliced lengthwise

1 stick butter
¼ cup Grand Marnier

♦ Cook the carrots in boiling water. Place the carrots in a food
  processor.
♦ Add the rest of ingredients and blend until smooth. Serve hot.

MINTED PEAS

Serves 8

4 pounds fresh peas
Rind from ½ orange, chopped
½ cup butter

¼ cup fresh mint, chopped
Salt and pepper

♦ Wash and shell the peas. Place 2 cups of water in a saucepan. Bring
  to a boil and add peas. Simmer the peas until tender.
♦ Melt the butter and add orange rind, fresh mint, salt and pepper. Pour
  over the peas.
♦ Serve immediately

ACORN SQUASH

Serves 4

2 large acorn squash
½ cup butter, melted

½ cup brown sugar

♦ Half the acorn squash and remove stems. In a pressure cooker, cook
  squash until tender. Remove and place the squash, pulp up in a
  baking dish.
♦ Pour melted butter into each squash center. Sprinkle with brown
  sugar.
♦ Bake at 350° for 20 minutes or butter is bubbling.

ACORN SQUASH SUPREME

Serves 4

2 medium acorn squash	½ cup heavy cream
1 tablespoon butter	½ cup maple syrup

- Preheat the oven to 350°.
- Place squash cut side up in greased baking dish. Brush the squash with butter.
- Combine the cream and syrup. Pour into the squash centers.
- Bake uncovered for 1 hour, or until tender.

Now Let Us Praise Fried Pies

CREAMED ONIONS

Serves 8

2 16 ounce jars small boiled onions (can also be purchased frozen)	¼ cup parmesan cheese

Sauce

1 stick butter	½ cup flour
2 cups half and half	

- Melt the butter in a saucepan. Stir in the flour. Gradually add half and half until thickened.
- Place the onions in a baking dish.
- Pour the sauce over the onions. Sprinkle with the parmesan cheese.
- Bake at 350° for ½ hour, until browned on top.

ONION TART

2 large Vidalia onions
¼ cup butter
2½ cups half and half
3 eggs

½ teaspoon ground nutmeg
1 cup grated Gruyere cheese
1 9" pie crust

- Preheat oven to 400°.
- Peel and thinly slice onions. Saute onions in butter in a skillet.
- Pour the onions into the pie crust and top with the cheese.
- In a bowl beat together half and half, nutmeg and eggs.
- Pour over the cheese.
- Bake for 35 minutes or until set and browned on top.

BAKED TOMATOES

Serves 4

2 large tomatoes
2 tablespoons basil, chopped
¼ cup fresh bread crumbs

¼ cup parmesan cheese
¼ cup melted butter

- Cut tomatoes in half.
- Combine the basil, bread crumbs and parmesan cheese in bowl.
- Spread the bread crumb mixture over the top of each tomato.
- Pour butter on top.
- Bake at 350° for 20 minutes, or until top is just browned.

STEWED TOMATOES

Serves 6

6 large tomatoes
½ cup butter

Salt and pepper
½ cup fresh basil

- Skin and dice the tomatoes. Put in a saucepan and cook for 5 minutes.
- Add the other ingredients and cook for 10 minutes.
- Serve hot.

TOMATO PUDDING

Serves 4

1 large can tomato puree   1 cup white bread cubes
1 cup brown sugar   ½ stick melted butter
¼ cup water

- ◆ In a saucepan boil the tomato puree, water and brown sugar for 5 minutes.
- ◆ Place the bread cubes in a one quart casserole dish.
- ◆ Pour the melted butter over the bread.
- ◆ Top with the tomato mixture.
- ◆ Bake at 375° for 30 minutes.

MASHED TURNIPS

Turnips whipped with white potatoes provide a delicious fall dish.

Serves 4-6

4 large potatoes   ½ cup milk
1 large turnip   Salt and pepper
¼ cup butter

- ◆ Peel and cut up the potatoes and turnip. Cook in boiling water until tender.
- ◆ In a bowl beat together potatoes, turnip, butter, milk and salt and pepper. Add more milk if too thick.
- ◆ Serve hot immediately.

CAULIFLOWER IN CHEESE SAUCE

Serves 6

1 head cauliflower
½ stick butter
¼ cup flour

1 cup milk
1 cup grated cheddar cheese

- ◆ Cook the whole cauliflower in a pressure cooker until tender.
- ◆ In a saucepan melt the butter, stir in the flour and gradually add the milk until thickened.
- ◆ Add the cheese.
- ◆ Pour the sauce over the cauliflower.
- ◆ Serve immediately.

EGGPLANT PARMIGIANA

Serves 6-8

1 cup olive oil
2 cloves garlic, minced
1 onion, chopped
1 32 ounce can tomatoes
1 tablespoon basil

1 cup flour
1 egg
2 eggplant
2 cups mozzarella cheese

- ◆ Heat ½ the olive oil in a skillet and add onion until transparent,
- ◆ Add garlic, tomatoes, basil, salt and pepper. Cook for 30 minutes. Pour into a bowl.
- ◆ Heat oven to 350°.
- ◆ Combine the egg and flour.
- ◆ Dip the eggplant slices in the flour.
- ◆ Pour the remaining oil into the skillet and heat until bubbling.
- ◆ Fry the eggplant in the skillet.
- ◆ In a casserole dish place alternating layers of eggplant, sauce and cheese.
- ◆ Bake for 30 minutes.

BLACK BEAN BURRITOS

Serves 4

½ cup green pepper, chopped
½ cup red pepper, chopped
2 tablespoons olive oil
1 small onion, chopped
2 cloves garlic, crushed

2 cups cooked rice
1 can black beans
2 teaspoons chili powder
Tortillas
1 cup cheddar cheese, grated

- ◆ Saute the green and red peppers, and onions in olive oil.
- ◆ Add the garlic, rice, chili powder, and black beans with bean juice.
- ◆ Spread ½ cup of the bean mixture down the center of each tortilla.
- ◆ Top with some of the grated cheese.
- ◆ Roll the tortilla around the filling.
- ◆ Transfer the burritos to a baking dish, seam side down.
- ◆ Cover the dish with foil and bake for 10-15 minutes, until heated. Transfer to warm plates.
- ◆ For a spicier burrito substitute hot pepper Monterey Jack cheese.
- ◆ For a quesadilla, fry the tortillas stuffed with the bean mixture in hot oil.

Sauce

1 15 ounce can tomato sauce
2 cloves garlic, crushed
2 jalapeno chiles

¼ cup onion, chopped
2 tablespoons coriander

- ◆ Cut the chile in quarters, remove the seeds and dice.
- ◆ Combine the ingredients in a saucepan. Simmer for 10-15 minutes.
- ◆ Serve the sauce over the burritos.

SALADS

Chesapeake Bay Oyster Tongers

Tomatoes Stuffed with Crab Meat
Herb Bread/Butter
Lemon Pie with Raspberries

TOMATOES STUFFED WITH CRAB

Serves 4

This is perfect for a lady's luncheon or a hot summer day.

1 pound crab meat
½ cup chopped celery
Juice of ½ lemon
½ cup mayonnaise

4 tomatoes
2 tablespoons onion, chopped
2 tablespoons basil, chopped
Lettuce

- ◆ Combine the ingredients, except for the lettuce and tomatoes.
- ◆ Core the tomato. Spoon the crab meat mixture into the tomato.
- ◆ Serve on a bed of lettuce. Garnish with lemon slices.
- ◆ Half an avocado can be substituted for the tomato.

WILTED LETTUCE

Serves 4-6

1 head of fresh garden lettuce
2 spring onions, chopped
6 slices bacon
4 hard boiled eggs, sliced

Salt and pepper, to taste
¼ cup vinegar

- ◆ Chop the lettuce fine with a liberal amount of spring onions. Sprinkle these with salt, pepper and vinegar.
- ◆ Fry the slices of bacon, saving the bacon fat. Crumble the bacon over top of the lettuce.
- ◆ Dribble hot bacon fat over salad to wilt lettuce. Garnish with egg slices.

Now Let Us Praise Fried Pies

COLE SLAW

Serves 8

1 large head of cabbage, shredded

Dressing

3 tablespoons sugar
1½ teaspoons flour
1 teaspoon dry mustard
1 egg
¾ cup milk

¼ cup vinegar
1 tablespoon butter
1 teaspoon mustard seed
1 teaspoon celery salt

- ◆ Cook the ingredients in a double boiler until thickened. Pour over the cabbage.
- ◆ Serve immediately in a salad bowl, or refrigerate.

BLUE CHEESE AND ENDIVE SALAD

Serves 8

1 large head romaine lettuce
1 pound endive

½ pound blue cheese
½ cup pecans or walnuts

- ◆ Break up the lettuce and endive into pieces in a large salad bowl.
- ◆ Crumble the blue cheese. Add cheese and walnuts to lettuce and endive.

Dressing

¼ cup balsamic vinegar
1 tablespoon Dijon mustard

¼ cup olive oil or walnut oil
¼ cup honey

- ◆ In a small bowl mix together all ingredients.
- ◆ You may not want to use all the dressing at this time, but it can be kept in a jar until further use.

CUCUMBER SALAD

Serves 8

3 medium cucumbers
¼ cup fresh dill

¼ cup vinegar
Salt and pepper

- ◆ Peel and slice the cucumbers.
- ◆ Place the cucumbers in a bowl with the vinegar, salt, pepper and dill.
- ◆ Let marinate overnight.

CUCUMBERS IN SOUR CREAM

Serves 6

2 large cucumbers, peeled and sliced
1 cup sour cream

½ teaspoon salt
1 teaspoon dill, chopped
¼ cup scallions, chopped

- ◆ In a large bowl combine the sour cream, salt, dill, and scallions.
- ◆ Add the cucumbers.
- ◆ Refrigerate before serving.
- ◆ Yogurt can be substituted for sour cream.

CUCUMBER AND TOMATO SALAD

Serves 6-8

4 large ripe tomatoes
2 medium cucumbers
¼ cup fresh basil, chopped
¼ cup fresh parsley, chopped

¼ cup scallions, chopped
¼ cup tarragon vinegar
½ cup olive oil
1 teaspoon salt

- ◆ Slice the tomatoes and cucumbers. Arrange on a platter.
- ◆ In a bowl combine the basil, parsley, scallions, vinegar, olive oil, and salt.
- ◆ Pour over cucumbers and tomatoes.

CUCUMBER MOUSSE

Serves 12

5 large cucumbers
2 cups ginger ale
2 packages lime gelatin
2 packages plain gelatin
Tabasco sauce- heavy splash

1 tablespoon sugar
1 cup sour cream
1 cup mayonnaise
Tomatoes

- ◆ Peel and grate the cucumbers. Drain for one hour. Add ½ the ginger ale.
- ◆ Heat the remainder of the ginger ale and dissolve the gelatins.
- ◆ Add to the cucumber mixture. Cool
- ◆ Mix in all other ingredients, except tomatoes.
- ◆ Pour into a large mold and chill until firm.
- ◆ Unmold, and serve on a platter and garnish with tomato slices.

Now Let Us Praise Fried Pies

SPINACH SALAD

Serves 4-6

1 pound fresh spinach
2 grapefruit, sectioned

1 small red onion, sliced

- ◆ Wash and drain the spinach.
- ◆ Place in a salad bowl. Add onion and grapefruit.

Dressing

2 tablespoons honey
2 tablespoons vinegar

¼ cup olive oil

- ◆ Combine the ingredients in bowl and pour over the salad.

SPINACH AND BACON SALAD

Serves 6

1 pound spinach
6 slices bacon

3 hard boiled eggs, sliced

- Wash and take stems off spinach. Place the spinach in a salad bowl.
- Cook the bacon and reserve the bacon fat. Crumble bacon.
- Add the bacon and eggs to the spinach.
- 1 cup croutons can also be added to this salad.
- Or 1 cup sliced mushrooms

Dressing

Leftover bacon fat
¼ cup vinegar
¼ cup sugar or honey

Salt and pepper to season
½ teaspoon poppy seeds

- In the skillet used to cook the bacon, combine the ingredients.
- Toss with the salad.

WATERCRESS SALAD WITH PEARS

Serves 4

2 bunches watercress
2 ripe pears, peeled, cored and
sliced
½ cup crumbled blue cheese

½ cup chopped pecans
¼ cup raspberry vinegar
¼ cup olive oil

- Snip the stems off the watercress.
- Place the watercress in a salad bowl and lay pears in a fan shape.
- Top with blue cheese and pecans.
- Sprinkle with vinegar and olive oil. Toss.

WATERCRESS SALAD WITH ORANGES

2 large bunches watercress
1 small red onion

1 can mandarin oranges or 2 oranges, peeled and sectioned

- ◆ Wash and take stems off watercress. Put in a salad bowl.
- ◆ Slice the onion.
- ◆ Drain the mandarin oranges.
- ◆ Add onion and oranges to watercress.

Dressing

2 tablespoons honey
2 tablespoons olive oil

2 tablespoons vinegar

- ◆ Combine all ingredients in a small bowl. Toss with the salad.

AVOCADO AND GRAPEFRUIT SALAD

Use fresh grapefruit for this when possible.

1 head Boston lettuce
2 large grapefruit, peeled and sectioned

1 large avocado, peeled and sliced

- ◆ Place the lettuce in salad bowl.
- ◆ Arrange the grapefruit sections and avocado in a fan around the lettuce.

Dressing

¼ cup walnut oil
¼ cup red wine vinegar

1 tablespoon sugar
1 tablespoon lemon juice

- ◆ Combine the ingredients in a small jar.
- ◆ Pour only enough over salad to lightly coat.

BEET SALAD

This salad goes particularly well with beef tenderloin or other meats cooked on a grill. A perfect summer salad with great color.

Serves 8

8 large beets
4 Tbls. balsamic vinegar
Zest of one orange
½ cup walnut oil
1 teaspoon coarse salt

¼ teaspoon black pepper
1 medium red onion, sliced
8 endive leaves
3 tablespoons toasted walnuts
¾ cup blue cheese

- Preheat an oven to 400°.
- Wrap the beets without their tops in tin foil and bake in oven 50 minutes, or until tender.
- After cooling the beets, remove the skins and slice into thin pieces.
- Combine the balsamic vinegar, orange rind, walnut oil, salt and pepper in a large bowl.
- Thinly slice the onion.
- Add the beets and onion to the bowl, toss, and let marinate for 30 or more minutes.
- On separate salad plates place a piece of endive. Spoon the beet mixture onto the endive. Sprinkle the beets with walnuts and blue cheese.
- This salad can also be served in a large bowl, without the endive, but still sprinkling the blue cheese and walnuts on top for color. A green salad bowl is a nice contrast to the beets.

BOURSIN POTATO SALAD

Can be served hot or cold

Serves 8

16 red bliss potatoes
4 green onions, chopped

1 cup sour cream
1 container Boursin cheese

- Cut potatoes into cubes, leaving skins on. Boil potatoes until tender.
- Combine all ingredients while the potatoes are still hot.
- Serve immediately.

POTATO SALAD WITH BLUE CHEESE

The small red bliss potatoes are the best for making potato salad. Leave the skins on for more flavor and color.

Serves 8-10

16 red bliss potatoes
½ cup white wine
1 cup mayonnaise
1 cup sour cream
½ pound blue cheese
1 small red onion

1 cup celery
2 tablespoons Dijon mustard
2 tablespoons white vinegar
Salt and pepper

- ◆ Cook the potatoes until tender. Cool and cut into one inch cubes.
- ◆ Chop the celery into small pieces and mince the onion in a bowl.
- ◆ Combine with the potatoes.
- ◆ Combine in a bowl the wine, mayonnaise, sour cream, mustard, and vinegar. Toss with the potato mixture.
- ◆ Crumble the blue cheese on top of the salad.

ELEANOR'S REUNION POTATO SALAD

8 servings

¼ cup French dressing
5 medium potatoes, cubed
1 cup celery, diced
¼ cup onion, chopped

4 hard boiled eggs, sliced
1 teaspoon salt
½ cup mayonnaise
1 teaspoon celery seed

- ◆ Boil the potatoes until tender. Place potatoes in a salad bowl.
- ◆ Pour French dressing over the potatoes. Chill 2 hours.
- ◆ Add celery, onion, eggs, salt, mayonnaise and celery seed, and mix carefully.
- ◆ Chill 4 hours.

Now Let Us Praise Fried Pies

TOMATO ASPIC WITH CRAB SALAD

Serves 6-8

2 envelopes plain gelatin
1 teaspoon sugar
4 cups tomato juice
Juice of one lemon
Salt and pepper
¼ cup chopped celery

1 avocado, sliced
3 cups crab meat salad
Lettuce
4 hard-boiled eggs, sliced
Parsley

- In a saucepan stir together the gelatin, sugar and 2 cups of the tomato juice. Stir over moderate heat until the gelatin dissolves.
- Add the rest of the tomato juice, lemon, salt and pepper.
- In a large round mold line the bottom with the celery and avocado.
- Pour in the tomato mix. Chill until firm.
- Turn out onto a serving platter lined with the lettuce.
- In the center place the crab meat salad. Garnish with the eggs and parsley.

KAY'S WINTER SALAD

Serves 8-10

2 medium heads lettuce
1 avocado, sliced
1½ cups cauliflower florets

2 tomatoes, sliced
1 cup toasted sliced almonds
1 garlic clove, halved

- Rub the salad bowl with the garlic. Add the other ingredients.

Salad Dressing

¾ cup vegetable oil
2 cloves garlic, crushed
¼ cup lemon juice
1 teaspoon sugar

Salt and pepper
½ teaspoon celery seeds
1 teaspoon paprika
1½ teaspoons dry mustard

- Blend all the ingredients in a food processor and place in a jar.
- When the salad is to be served, pour the dressing over the salad ingredients. Serve immediately.

CHICKEN SALAD WITH GRAPES

Serves 4

2 cups cooked chicken
1 cup green seedless grapes
½ cup chopped celery
¼ cup pecans or walnuts

1 tablespoon curry powder
¼ cup mayonnaise
¼ cup sour cream
Lettuce

- Combine all the ingredients in a bowl.
- Serve on a bed of lettuce on a platter, or on individual salad plates.

CHICKEN SALAD ALMONDINE

Serves 4

2 cups cooked chicken
1 large can artichoke hearts, quartered
¼ cup scallion, chopped
Salt and pepper

1 tablespoon lemon juice
¾ cup mayonnaise
¼ cup toasted almonds
Lettuce

- Combine the chicken, artichokes, green onion, salt and pepper, lemon juice and mayonnaise in a bowl.
- Cover and refrigerate for at least one hour before serving.
- Place the chicken salad on separate lettuce leaves and garnish with the almonds.

CURRIED CHICKEN SALAD

Serves 4

2 cups cooked chicken
½ cup peanuts
½ cup raisins
½ cup coconut

¾ cup mayonnaise
1 tablespoon curry
1 teaspoon ginger
4 large Boston lettuce leaves

- Combine all the ingredients in a bowl, except lettuce.
- Refrigerate for at least one hour.
- Serve on separate lettuce leaves with mango chutney.

CHICKEN PESTO SALAD

Serves 4

2 cooked large boneless chicken
breasts
½ pound linguini

½ cup pesto sauce
Grated parmesan cheese

- ♦ Cook linguine according to instructions.
- ♦ Cut chicken up into small pieces.
- ♦ Toss the chicken with linguine and pesto.
- ♦ Serve hot or cold with grated cheese.

CAESAR SALAD

Serves 6

1 large head romaine lettuce
3 cloves garlic, crushed
Juice of one lemon
1 cup fresh croutons
1 can anchovies

1 egg
¼ cup parmesan Cheese
¼ cup olive oil
Salt and pepper

- ♦ Rub the crushed garlic around the sides of a large salad bowl. Add salt and pepper, lemon juice and olive oil.
- ♦ Tear the lettuce into bite-size pieces and add to the bowl.
- ♦ Add the anchovies and break an egg over the salad.
- ♦ Sprinkle the croutons on top and then the grated cheese.
- ♦ Serve immediately.

Use the Caesar Salad recipe but add one of the following for a hearty meal.

- ♦ 2 pounds grilled chicken, cut up into small cubes
- ♦ 2 dozen fried oysters
- ♦ 2 pounds fresh crab meat
- ♦ 2 pounds cooked shrimp
- ♦ 2 pounds grilled rockfish
- ♦ 2 pounds sliced grilled steak

PASTA SALAD

Serves 8-10

1 package shell pasta
1 cup broccoli florets
½ cup red pepper, chopped
½ cup green pepper, chopped
¼ cup red onion, chopped
½ cup carrots, sliced

½ cup celery, sliced
1 cup black olives
¼ cup fresh basil, chopped
¼ cup white wine vinegar
¼ cup olive oil
Salt and pepper

- Cook pasta according to directions. Drain and place in a large bowl.
- Add all the other ingredients and toss.
- Refrigerate at least one hour before serving.
- For a heartier salad:
- Add 4 sliced eggs; 2 cans tuna fish; 1 pound fresh crab meat; or two cups grilled chicken.

CARROT SALAD

Serves 4

4 large carrots, peeled
½ cup raisins

½ cup toasted almonds
¼ cup mayonnaise

- Grate the carrots and place in a bowl. Add other ingredients.
- Toss and serve in a salad bowl.

WALDORF SALAD

Serves 4

4 apples, peeled cored and sliced
½ cup celery, chopped

¼ cup mayonnaise
¼ cup walnuts or pecans

- Combine all ingredients in a bowl.
- Serve on a bed of lettuce.

Beef Tenderloin
Yorkshire Pudding
Brussels Sprouts
Bing Cherry Salad
Pot de Creme

BING CHERRY SALAD

2 envelopes raspberry Jello
1½ cups boiling water
1 can pitted bing cherries

8 ounces cream cheese
½ cup pecans

- Dissolve the Jello in boiling water.
- Pour the Bing cherries into a ring mold, saving the juice. Add juice to the Jello.
- Make small balls out of the cream cheese and add to the mold along with the pecans.
- Pour the Jello over mold. Refrigerate until firm.
- Unmold and serve on a plate.
- Garnish with mayonnaise and mint leaves.

LAYERED SALAD

Serves 12

1 large head iceberg lettuce
1 bunch scallions, diced
½ cup green pepper, chopped
½ cup celery, chopped
½ cup red pepper, chopped

1 pound fresh green peas
1 cup shredded Monterey Jack cheese
1 cup mayonnaise
8 slices bacon, crumbled

- Layer the first 7 ingredients in a glass salad bowl.
- Spread the mayonnaise over the cheese.
- Top with the bacon.
- Refrigerate covered overnight.

WALNUT GREENS SALAD

Serves 8-10

1 pkg. mixed spring greens
1 cup walnuts, toasted

1 cup mushrooms
½ cup blue cheese, crumbled

♦ Combine the ingredients in a large salad bowl.

Dressing

¼ cup walnut oil
2 Tbls. balsamic vinegar

1 tablespoon Dijon mustard
2 teaspoons sugar

♦ Combine all the ingredients in a small bowl and pour over the greens.

BIBB LETTUCE SALAD

Serves 4-6

2 heads bibb lettuce
½ pound brie, sliced

2 cups French bread croutons

♦ In a salad bowl arrange the bibb lettuce
♦ Top with brie and croutons.

French Bread Croutons

2 cups French bread, cubed
½ stick butter, melted

1 teaspoon garlic salt

♦ Place the bread in a baking dish. Cover with butter and garlic salt.
♦ Bake in 350° oven for about 10 minutes, or until toasted.

Dressing

¼ cup olive oil
Juice of ½ lemon

Freshly grated pepper

♦ In a bowl combine the oil and lemon.
♦ Pour over the salad. Season with fresh pepper.

PASTAS AND RICE

Skipjack – Annapolis, Maryland

BASIC RISOTTO

Risotto takes about a half hour to prepare, but it is worth the effort. It can be served as a rice dish or on its own by adding peas, mushrooms, ham, shrimp, lobster, cooked turkey or chicken.

3-4 servings

1 cup risotto
1½ cups hot chicken broth
1 tablespoon green onion

1 tablespoon butter
Fresh grated Parmesan or
Asiago cheese

- In saucepan melt butter and add chopped onion.
- Stir in the rice.
- Very slowly stir in ¼ cup broth at a time, until all is used.
- The rice should be tender.
- Serve with grated cheese.

RISOTTO WITH CRAB MEAT

- Prepare the Basic Risotto recipe, but before serving add 1 pound crab meat. Top with grated cheese.

RISOTTO PRIMAVERA

Serves 6

- Prepare the Basic Risotto recipe.
- Steam ½ pound fresh spinach, ¼ pound fresh green peas, ½ pound asparagus, and ¼ cup fresh chopped parsley.
- This is also good with broccoli.
- Add vegetables to the risotto

RISOTTO WITH MUSHROOMS

- Prepare the Basic Risotto recipe.
- Just before serving add ½ pound sliced Portabello mushrooms that have been sauteed in butter. Dribble with a small amount of truffle oil.

COUSCOUS

Serves 4

1 tablespoon butter
1½ cups chicken broth
1 cup couscous
2 Tbls. green chiles, chopped
2 tablespoons pine nuts

2 tablespoons lemon juice
2 Tbls. fresh parsley, chopped
1 teaspoon chili powder
¼ cup olive oil

- ◆ In a saucepan melt the butter and add the broth. Bring to a boil and add the couscous.
- ◆ Remove from the heat and let stand for 5 minutes, covered.
- ◆ Add chile peppers, pine nuts, parsley, salt and pepper.
- ◆ Then mix in chili powder, olive oil and lemon juice.
- ◆ This is very good served with lamb.

WILD RICE WITH MUSHROOMS

1 pound wild rice
4 cups chicken broth
½ cup celery, diced

½ cup onions, chopped
½ pound mushrooms, sliced
Salt and pepper to taste

- ◆ Preheat oven to 350°.
- ◆ In a large casserole combine all the ingredients.
- ◆ Bake in an oven for about 1½ hours.

WILD RICE ALMONDINE

Serves 4

1 cup wild rice
½ pound mushrooms, sliced
3 tablespoons onion, minced

½ cup almonds, sliced
3 cups chicken broth
½ cup butter

- ◆ Combine the ingredients in a baking dish.
- ◆ Bake 1 hour at 350°.
- ◆ ½ cup sliced water chestnuts or pecans can be substituted for the almonds.

RED BEANS AND RICE

Serves 4-6

1 cup dried red beans
2 cups chicken broth
1 cup drained tomatoes
¾ cup water
1 Tbls. Worcestershire sauce
4 bay leaves

½ tsp. cayenne or Tabasco
½ teaspoon salt
1 small onion, chopped
2 cups uncooked rice
¼ pound bacon, chopped
3 cloves garlic, crushed

- ♦ Put the beans in a bowl and cover with boiling water. Let stand 2 hours. Drain.
- ♦ In a large ovenproof dish combine the broth, rice, tomatoes, water, Worcestershire sauce, bay leaves, salt and cayenne. Bring to a boil and add the beans. Stir in the onion, garlic and bacon.
- ♦ Cover the pan and cook in the oven for 1½ hours at 350°.
- ♦ Serve with chicken or pork.

RICE WITH PECANS

Serves 8

2 cups rice
2 cups chicken stock

1 cup pecans
1 cup raisins

- ♦ Cook rice with stock in a saucepan. When tender add pecans and raisins.
- ♦ This is good served with turkey, chicken, duck or goose.

RICE AND PEAS

Serves 4

1 cup rice
1 pound fresh peas

2 tablespoons butter
1 tablespoon mint

- ♦ Cook the rice according to instructions.
- ♦ Add the peas, butter and mint. This can be served hot or cold.

SPINACH PASTA AND GORGONZOLA

Serves 6

1 pound spinach linguine
1 can artichoke hearts

½ cup cream
½ pound Gorgonzola, crumbled

- ♦ Cook the linguine according to instructions. Drain.
- ♦ Drain the artichoke hearts.
- ♦ In saucepan combine the linguine, artichoke hearts, and cream.
- ♦ Sprinkle Gorgonzola on top.
- ♦ Serve immediately.

FETTUCCINE ALFREDO

Serves 4

1 pound fettuccine
8 slices bacon, cooked
2 cloves garlic, crushed

1 cup heavy cream
¼ cup parsley, chopped
Grated parmesan cheese

- ♦ Cook the fettuccine according to the directions. Remove from pan.
- ♦ Heat the cream and garlic in the pan, but do not boil.
- ♦ Add the pasta, bacon, and parsley.
- ♦ Serve hot with parmesan cheese.

BREADS, BISCUITS, AND COFFEE CAKES

Cinnamon Coffee Cake – Mount Clare Mansion

There are a number of old mills near the Chesapeake, many still grinding corn into flour and cornmeal. The first gristmill was built in Jamestown, Virginia in 1621 to mill flour from wheat. Wye Mill, Wye Mills, Maryland dates from c1682 and is probably the oldest building still standing in Maryland. The mill has served as the boundary between Talbot and Queen Anne's Counties since 1706. In 1706 Richard Sweatman operated a sawmill and two gristmills here. Edward Lloyd controlled the mill from 1722 to 1793. Col. William Hemsley operated the mill for Mr. Lloyd and eventually owned it, having married Maria Lloyd, daughter of Edward Lloyd IV. The mill produced cornmeal for Gen. Washington's Continental Army at Valley Forge in 1778. The flour was ordered and paid for by Robert Morris of Oxford, Maryland. Alexander Hemsley sold the property to Samuel Hopkins in 1821 for $4,000. The state of Maryland eventually bought the mill. It was deeded to the Friends of Wye Mill in 1996. There is only one gristmill operating today, still producing cornmeal and flour.

In 1780 Oliver Evans of Delaware invented a water-driven vertical conveyor belt for automating flour mills. He received a patent for his mill in 1791.

Other old mills include one at Cyrus McCormick Farm in Raphine, Virginia. Cyrus McCormick invented the mechanized reaper, that forever changed farming. However, Obed Hussey of Baltimore invented a mechanical reaper one year before Cyrus McCormick.

Tuckahoe is a marsh plant whose roots were used by the Indians to make bread. Tuckahoe was also called Indian bread or loaf.

PUMPKIN BREAD

2 cups flour
1½ cups sugar
1 teaspoon baking soda
½ teaspoon salt
1 cup pumpkin
1 teaspoon cinnamon

1 teaspoon nutmeg
1 teaspoon allspice
½ teaspoon ground cloves
½ teaspoon ginger
½ cup vegetable oil
2 eggs

- Preheat oven to 350°.
- Combine the ingredients in a bowl and pour into a greased loaf pan.
- Bake 1 hour.
- This is good served with cream cheese.

150

SOUR CREAM COFFEE CAKE

This sour cream coffee cake is our favorite. If covered and put in the refrigerator, it will stay fresh for two weeks. Just cut in squares and warm up in the oven for a few minutes.

1 stick butter
1 cup sugar
2 eggs
1 cup sour cream

1½ teaspoons baking powder
1½ cups flour
1 teaspoon vanilla

- ◆ Melt butter in a large saucepan on low heat.
- ◆ Beat in sugar, eggs, sour cream, baking powder, flour and vanilla.
- ◆ Pour into a 9 inch square baking dish.
- ◆ During the fall and winter add sliced apples or pears to the batter. During the summer blueberries or sliced peaches are a delicious addition.

Topping

¼ cup sugar
¼ cup brown sugar

¼ cup walnuts or pecans
¼ cup coconut

- ◆ Mix the topping ingredients together and spoon over batter.
- ◆ Bake at 350° for 45 minutes.
- ◆ To make blueberry muffins use the same recipe as the sour cream coffee cake and add one pint blueberries. Pour into muffin tins. Bake 35 minutes at 350°.

POPOVERS

2 eggs
1 cup milk

1 cup flour
½ teaspoon salt

- ◆ Break the eggs into a bowl.
- ◆ Add milk, flour and salt. Mix well with a spoon.
- ◆ Pour batter into greased muffin tins ¾ full.
- ◆ Turn on the oven to 450°. Bake 30 minutes.
- ◆ The secret to making popovers is using a cold oven and not opening it while the popovers are baking.

EASY FRENCH BREAD

3 cups flour
1 cup warm water
1 package yeast

1 tablespoon olive oil
½ teaspoon salt

- ◆ Dissolve the yeast in the cup of warm water.
- ◆ Put the flour in a food processor and slowly add the yeast and other ingredients till a ball is formed.
- ◆ Place the ball in an oiled large bowl and cover with a clean cloth. Set in warm place and let rise for one hour, until at least doubled in size.
- ◆ On an oiled cookie sheet, sprinkled with cornmeal, shape the dough into a long loaf. Let rise one more hour.
- ◆ Preheat the oven to 500°.
- ◆ Bake the bread for 15 minutes or until golden in color.
- ◆ Serve warm with butter.
- ◆ 1 Tbls. rosemary can be added for additional flavor

HERB CHEESE BREAD

1 teaspoon sugar
1 package dry yeast
¼ cup warm water
½ cup parmesan cheese
2¼ cups flour

1 tablespoon butter
1 teaspoon mixed herbs
¼ - ½ cup heavy cream
½ teaspoon salt

- ◆ Dissolve the sugar and yeast in warm water.
- ◆ Place all the ingredients, starting with only ¼ cup cream and adding more if too dry, in food processor and process until a ball forms.
- ◆ Place in oiled bowl and cover.
- ◆ Let rise in a warm place until doubled, about 2 hours.
- ◆ Punch down and then let rest for 5 minutes.
- ◆ Oil a bread loaf pan and shape dough into pan.
- ◆ Cover and let rise until doubled, approximately 50-60 minutes.
- ◆ Bake at 375° for 35 minutes, or until browned.

CHEESE HERB BREAD

Serves 6

1 teaspoon sugar
1¼ cups lukewarm water
1 envelope dry yeast
3 cups flour
1 teaspoon salt

1 teaspoon dry mustard
¼ teaspoon ground pepper
3 teaspoons chives
4 tablespoons fresh parsley
2 cups cheddar cheese

- Dissolve the sugar and yeast in the lukewarm water in a mixing bowl. Let sit for 10-15 minutes.
- Add the flour, mustard, salt and pepper. Then stir in the chives, parsley and 1 ½ cups cheese.
- Knead the dough on a flour surface, or place in food processor.
- Butter the bowl and place back into the bowl. Let rise for one hour or until doubled in size.
- Knead for 5 minutes, or place again in food processor.
- Place in a buttered loaf pan. Let rise once again until doubled in size.
- Sprinkle the rest of the cheese over the loaf.
- Place in oven warmed to 375° for 45 minutes, and browned on top.

BANANA BREAD

Makes one loaf

3 large ripe bananas
1 egg, well beaten
1 cup sugar
3 tablespoons melted butter

2 cups flour
1 teaspoon baking soda
1 teaspoon baking powder
½ teaspoon salt

- Preheat oven to 350°.
- Mash the bananas in a bowl.
- Beat in egg and sugar.
- Add melted butter and dry ingredients.
- Bake in a greased loaf pan for one hour.

NUTTY BANANA BREAD

Even though bananas don't come from this region, I still remember my mother making this with very ripe bananas. The bread is delicious served sliced, with cream cheese.

2 cups sugar
1 cup butter
6 very ripe bananas, mashed
4 eggs, beaten

2½ cups flour
1 teaspoon salt
2 teaspoons baking powder
½ cup pecans or walnuts

- ◆ Preheat the oven to 350°.
- ◆ In a bowl cream the butter and sugar.
- ◆ Add the bananas and eggs. Then beat in the flour, salt, baking powder and nuts. Blend well.
- ◆ Pour into a loaf pan. Bake 45-50 minutes.

JALAPENO CORNBREAD

2 cups flour
2 teaspoons baking powder
½ teaspoon salt
1 tablespoon sugar
2 cups cornmeal

2 eggs
2 cups buttermilk or milk
6 tablespoons melted butter
2 jalapeno chiles, seeded and minced

- ◆ Preheat the oven to 425°.
- ◆ Grease a large iron skillet and heat in oven.
- ◆ Beat together the egg, buttermilk and butter in a bowl. Add the dry ingredients. Pour into heated skillet.
- ◆ Bake until browned about 20-25 minutes.
- ◆

SPOON BREAD

½ stick butter
3 ears corn
3 cups milk
1 teaspoon salt

1 cup cornmeal
3 eggs
1 tablespoon sugar

- ◆ Preheat the oven to 350°.
- ◆ Spread 1 tablespoon butter over the sides of a casserole dish.
- ◆ Using a grater shred the corn into a saucepan saving the juice. Add 2 cups of the milk and bring to a boil. Slowly pour in the cornmeal, stirring constantly until thickened.
- ◆ Remove from heat and stir in rest of butter, milk and beat in egg yolks, sugar, and cayenne.
- ◆ Beat the egg whites until peaks are formed. Fold the egg whites into the corn mixture.
- ◆ Pour into the buttered casserole and bake 45 minutes.
- ◆ Serve immediately.

BISCUITS

These just melt in your mouth.

Makes 6-8 biscuits

6 tablespoons butter, softened
2 cups flour
¾ cup half and half

2 teaspoons baking powder
½ teaspoon salt

- ◆ Preheat oven to 450°.
- ◆ Put the butter in a food processor and soften. Add flour, baking powder and salt. Slowly add half and half.
- ◆ On floured cutting board gently pat down the dough.
- ◆ Using a small lip glass or round cutter, cut dough into round shapes and place on a cookie sheet.
- ◆ Bake 10 minutes or until just browned.
- ◆ Another version of this is to add ½ cup sharp cheddar cheese.
- ◆ One time when I forgot to get milk I used ½ cup sour cream and ¼ cup of water.

BEATEN BISCUITS

Beaten biscuits have been a tradition since early colonial times.

4 cups flour   1 teaspoon salt
1 tablespoon lard   1-2 cups water

- Sift together the flour and salt.
- Work the lard in with your fingers.
- Slowly add the water until a stiff dough is formed. Keep kneading the dough for at least thirty minutes, or more.
- Make small balls out of the dough, and flatten on a board with a rolling pin. Prick each biscuit with the tongs of a fork.
- Bake at 400° for 20 minutes. Serve hot.

HUSH PUPPIES

Makes about 20

¼ cup flour   ¾ cup buttermilk
4 teaspoons baking powder   1 tablespoon onion, onion
½ teaspoon salt   1 clove garlic, crushed
1½ cups white cornmeal   Vegetable oil
2 eggs

- Combine the flour, baking powder, salt and cornmeal. Add the eggs and buttermilk. If the batter is too thick add more milk. Beat in onion and garlic.
- In a large skillet pour oil until 2 to 3 inches deep. Heat the pan, but make sure the oil is hot, but not smoking.
- To make the hush puppies, take spoonfuls of batter and make a ball.
- Fry until brown, turning frequently.
- Keep warm in the oven. Serve hot.
- For a spicier hush puppy add 2 jalapeno peppers, seeded and minced to the batter
- Or ½ teaspoon cayenne

GARLIC BREAD

1 loaf Italian or French bread
½ stick butter
¼ cup olive oil

6 cloves garlic, minced
½ cup parmesan cheese

- ◆ Cut bread into slices, figuring at least two slices per person.
- ◆ Rub the bread slices with garlic.
- ◆ Pour some of the olive oil in to the skillet. Heat and add some of the butter Place bread in a skillet and brown on each side.
- ◆ Sprinkle with grated parmesan cheese.

RON'S CINNAMON STICKS

This is one of the most delicious treats for a special breakfast or a lady's tea. You can't eat just one of these!

1 unsliced loaf of white bread
2 sticks butter

1 cup sugar
¼ cup cinnamon

- ◆ Heat the oven to 300°.
- ◆ Cut the crusts off the bread. Cut into 4x1x1 oblong pieces.
- ◆ Melt the butter and add the brown sugar.
- ◆ Dip the bread sticks into the butter and then into sugar mixture. Place the sticks on a cookie sheet.
- ◆ Bake in the oven for 30 minutes or until crisp.

BRAN MUFFINS

1¼ cups flour
½ teaspoon salt
1 tablespoon baking powder
1 cup raisins
2 cups bran

¼ cup milk
½ stick butter
¼ cup brown sugar
1 egg
¼ cup sugar

- ◆ Preheat the oven to 400°.
- ◆ Mix together all the ingredients. Pour into greased muffin tins.
- ◆ Bake for 20-25 minutes.
- ◆ Dates can be substituted for the raisins. Nuts can also be added.

DILL BREAD

1 package dry yeast
1 cup warm water
1 tablespoon sugar
1 cup cottage cheese
1 tablespoon minced onion
2 teaspoons dill seed

2 tablespoons butter
2¼ cups flour
1 teaspoon salt
¼ teaspoon baking soda
1 egg

- Dissolve the yeast in the cup of water and add sugar.
- In a bowl combine all the other ingredients.
- Combine two mixtures.
- Let rise in greased bowl 30-50 minutes or until doubled in size.
- Put in a loaf pan and brush with butter.
- Bake 40-50 minutes at 350°

PORTUGUESE BREAD

Having some Nantucket blood in me, I have to include Portuguese bread. We serve this warm with butter. This is especially good with clam chowder or lobsters, and for sandwiches too.

2 tablespoon sugar
3 teaspoons salt
1 cup boiling water
1 package dry yeast

1 cup warm water
6 Tbls. vegetable shortening
6 cups flour
Olive oil

- Place sugar, salt and shortening in a bowl. Add boiling water. Cool to lukewarm
- Dissolve yeast in 1 cup lukewarm water. Add to sugar and shortening mixture.
- Add 3 cups of the flour and beat until smooth. Gradually add remaining flour. Knead the dough.
- Grease a bowl with olive oil. Place the dough in the bowl and put in a warm spot until dough is doubled in size.
- Punch down the dough and divide in half. Shape each into a round loaf and put on an oiled cookie sheet. Cover and let rise until doubled. Bake at 400° until golden.

EGG AND BRUNCH DISHES

Workboat - St. Michael's, Maryland

CRAB BENEDICT

Serves 4

3 egg yolks
1 stick butter, melted
¼ cup lemon juice
4 English muffins
8 hard boiled eggs, sliced

1 pound crab meat
½ pound asparagus, blanched and cut in inch slices

- ♦ In a food processor combine the egg yolks and slowly add the butter, then lemon juice to make the Hollandaise.
- ♦ Cut the English muffins in half and toast. Top with eggs, several pieces of asparagus on each English muffin and then spread crab meat over.
- ♦ Top with sauce. Serve immediately.

EGGS BENEDICT

Serves 4

8 hard-boiled eggs, sliced
4 English muffins
½ pound Canadian bacon

3 egg yolks
1 stick butter
¼ cup lemon juice

- ♦ In a food processor put the egg yolks and slowly add the butter, then lemon juice.
- ♦ Cut the English muffins in half and toast.
- ♦ Place sliced bacon on each English muffin and top with sliced eggs.
- ♦ Top with sauce. Serve immediately.
- ♦ Poached eggs can be substituted for hardboiled eggs.

160

TOMATO TART

4 plum tomatoes
½ cup grated cheddar cheese
2½ cups half and half

3 eggs
¼ cup fresh basil, chopped
9 inch pie crust

- ◆ Preheat the oven to 400°. Warm pie crust for 10 minutes. Remove from oven.
- ◆ Finely chop the tomatoes and place in the pie crust. Cover with the cheese and the basil.
- ◆ Beat together the eggs and the half and half.
- ◆ Pour the egg mixture over cheese. Bake 40 minutes or until set.

ONION PIE

1 cup Vidalia onion, sliced
2½ cups half and half
3 eggs

½ teaspoon nutmeg
1 cup Swiss cheese
9 inch pie crust

- ◆ Preheat oven to 350°.
- ◆ In a bowl beat together the half and half, nutmeg and eggs.
- ◆ Sprinkle onions in pie shell. Pour the egg mixture over the onions.
- ◆ Bake pie 45 minutes.
- ◆ 1 cup Gruyere cheese can be substituted for the Swiss cheese.

QUICHE LORRAINE

6 strips bacon, crumbled
1 cup Gruyere or Swiss cheese
3 eggs
2½ cups half and half

¼ teaspoon nutmeg
Salt and pepper to taste
1 9 inch pie crust

- ◆ Heat oven to 450°.
- ◆ Cook bacon until crisp.
- ◆ In the pie shell place crumbled bacon, then cheese.
- ◆ In a mixing bowl beat the eggs, half and half, nutmeg and salt and pepper. Pour over the cheese and bacon.
- ◆ Turn oven down to 350° and bake quiche 45 minutes until set.

May Day Luncheon

Crab Meat Quiche
Mixed Greens with Walnut Dressing
Blueberry Muffins
Fresh Strawberries with Rum Whipped Cream

CRAB MEAT QUICHE

Serves 4

1 9 inch pie crust
2½ cups half and half
3 eggs

½ pound crab meat
1 cup Gruyere cheese, grated
¼ cup scallions, chopped

- In a mixing bowl beat eggs and half and half.
- In a pie crust put in a layer of the Gruyere cheese and then crab meat and scallions. Pour the egg mixture over top.
- Bake 40 minutes at 400°.
- Swiss or Jarlsberg cheese can be substituted for the Gruyere.

CHEESE SOUFFLE

Serves 4

½ stick butter
¼ cup flour
1 cup half and half

1 cup grated cheddar cheese
4 eggs

- Preheat the oven to 350°.
- Melt the butter, and stir in the flour and slowly add the milk until thickened. Add the cheese.
- Separate the eggs and beat the egg whites until stiff. Add the egg yolks to the cheese mixture. Fold in the egg whites.
- Pour into a souffle dish.
- Bake for 45 minutes. Do not open oven. Serve immediately.
- For variety add one package cooked spinach or broccoli, 1 cup ham or chicken.

Easter Brunch

Creamed Chipped Beef
English Muffins
Fresh Strawberries
Hot Cross Buns

CREAMED CHIPPED BEEF

Serves 4

8 hard-boiled eggs
8 ounce package chipped beef
2 cups half and half

½ cup flour
1 stick butter

- In a saucepan melt the butter.
- Slowly add the flour, and then half and half till thickened.
- Stir in sliced eggs and chipped beef.
- Serve over toasted English muffins.
- For a little variety, add 1 can artichoke hearts, drained.

SAUSAGE AND CHEESE CASSEROLE

Serves 6-8

16 slices French or Italian bread
½ pound grated cheddar cheese
1 pound Smithfield ham sausage

6 eggs
2½ cups half and half
1 teaspoon dry mustard

- Cut the bread into small cubes.
- Brown sausage in a skillet, and crumble.
- In a 12 x 9 casserole dish place bread, then a layer of grated cheese and Smithfield ham sausage.
- Beat together the eggs, half and half, and mustard. Pour over the sausage mixture.
- Refrigerate overnight.
- Bake at 350° for 40-45 minutes until the casserole is set.
-

CREAMED EGGS

We like to serve these on cold winter Sundays or Easter morning.

Serves 4

1 stick butter
½ cup flour
2 cups half and half

8 hard-boiled eggs, sliced
4 English muffins

- ◆ In a saucepan melt the butter.
- ◆ Slowly add the flour, and then half and half till thickened.
- ◆ Stir in the sliced eggs.
- ◆ Serve over toasted English muffins.

ROLLUPS

While growing up this was our favorite breakfast besides waffles, "Flyaway Pancakes", and coffee cakes. Rollups are really French pancakes, and can be served with jams, honey or just butter and syrup.

For a family of five

4 eggs
1¼ cups milk
1½ cups flour
1 teaspoon salt

2/3 cup water
1 teaspoon vanilla
2 teaspoons baking powder
4 tablespoons powdered sugar

- ◆ Beat together the eggs, milk, water and vanilla.
- ◆ Add the dry ingredients, stirring to just slightly mix together.
- ◆ Heat a large skillet with a small amount of butter. Pour a large spoonful of batter in pan, spreading evenly.
- ◆ Unless you have two skillets these can only be done one at a time. We use an electric skillet placed on the table to speed up the process and keep everyone talking. Serve with butter and roll up the pancake.
- ◆ Pour syrup or honey over the roll-up.

WAFFLES

Makes six waffles

3 eggs
1½ cups milk
1¾ cups flour

2 teaspoons baking powder
¼ cup sugar
4 tablespoons melted butter

- ◆ Heat the waffle iron, while making this recipe.
- ◆ Separate the eggs. Beat together the yolks and milk. Add the dry ingredients.
- ◆ Beat the egg whites until stiff. Fold the egg whites in with the other ingredients.
- ◆ Pour the batter by large spoonfuls into the waffle iron. Be careful not to get too close to the side. Cook until brown.
- ◆ Serve the waffles with butter, syrup or honey.

FLYAWAY PANCAKES

- ◆ Makes about 8 small pancakes.

1 cup flour
¼ teaspoon salt
¼ cup sugar
1 tablespoon baking powder

1 egg
1 cup milk
¼ cup sour cream
2 tablespoons melted butter

- ◆ In bowl beat egg, milk and sour cream. Add salt, sugar, baking powder, flour, then butter.
- ◆ Pour the batter by large spoonfuls into a skillet and cook about 4 minutes to a side.
- ◆ Serve with butter and maple syrup.

GERMAN PANCAKES

When our family gathered on Long Island for Christmas we would go into Luchow's in New York City for dinner. Luchow's had a huge Christmas tree and an "oompah band". For dessert we would share German pancakes, if we had any room left.

8 pancakes

6 large eggs
2 teaspoons baking powder
½ teaspoon salt
2 cups milk

1 tablespoon sugar
1 stick butter
1½ cups water

♦ Separate the eggs. Beat the yolks with the rest of the ingredients in a bowl.
♦ Beat the egg whites until stiff, and fold into the yolk mixture. Let stand 30 minutes.
♦ In a 10 inch skillet melt 2 tablespoons butter.
♦ Pour in ½ cup of the batter. Cook over medium heat covered for about 5 minutes, adjusting heat if too hot. Cook until puffed up and browned.
♦ Serve with cinnamon and sugar, lemon juice and lingonberry jam with the pancakes rolled up.

POTATO PANCAKES

These can be served with pork, applesauce, and red cabbage.

Serves 6

3 pounds potatoes, peeled
4 eggs
1¼ cups flour

½ cup onion, chopped
1 teaspoon salt
Oil

♦ Place the potatoes in a food processor and grate. Add the eggs, flour, onion and salt.
♦ Heat oil in a large skillet.
♦ Spoon about ½ cup potato mixture into hot oil. Brown on each side.
♦ Keep warm in oven until ready to serve.

SCRAMBLED EGGS WITH CRAB

Serves 4

2 cups crab meat
8 eggs
½ teaspoon salt
¼ teaspoon pepper

2 tablespoons scallions, chopped
2 tablespoons butter
Parsley

- ◆ Beat the eggs with the salt, pepper and scallions in a bowl.
- ◆ In a skillet heat the butter and add the eggs. Scramble the eggs.
- ◆ When the eggs are just about set, add the crab meat until heated.
- ◆ Serve immediately.
- ◆ Gruyere Cheese can also be added.

SUNDAY MORNING OMELET

2 servings

4 eggs
½ cup grated cheddar cheese

1 tablespoon chopped parsley
Butter

- ◆ Beat the eggs in a bowl.
- ◆ Heat a skillet and add 2 tablespoons butter. Pour in the eggs. With a spatula scrape the sides of the pan to keep from sticking.
- ◆ When set, sprinkle the cheese and parsley over the eggs.
- ◆ Carefully slide the omelet onto a cutting board so that it is folded in half.
- ◆ Let sit for 1-2 minutes. Cut in half.
- ◆ ¼ cup chopped ham can also be added.

SPANISH OMELET

Serves 2

4 eggs
1 tomato, chopped finely
¼ cup yellow pepper, chopped
1 green chile, chopped finely

2 Tbls. onion, chopped
4 black olives, sliced
Butter

- ◆ Beat the eggs.
- ◆ Heat the skillet and add 2 tablespoons butter. Pour in the eggs. With a spatula scrape the sides of the pan to keep from sticking.
- ◆ When set, sprinkle the vegetables over the eggs.
- ◆ Carefully slide the omelet onto a cutting board so that it is folded in half.
- ◆ Let sit for 1-2 minutes. Cut in half.
- ◆ ¼ cup grated cheddar cheese can also be added with the vegetables.

FRENCH OMELET

French omelet pans have two sides so that they can be folded together. This is an elegant and light dish that needs to be served immediately. Do not add cheese or other omelet ingredients as this is delicate and can stand on its own.

2 servings

4 eggs
1 teaspoon baking powder

¼ cup milk

- ◆ Separate the eggs. Beat the yolks, milk and baking powder together.
- ◆ In another bowl beat the egg whites until stiff. Fold into the yolk mixture.
- ◆ Heat the omelet pan and put one tablespoon butter in each side. When butter is bubbling add egg mixture to each side.
- ◆ Scrape the pan sides to keep from sticking.
- ◆ After it has risen carefully fold one side of pan over other. Cook for about 4 minutes and then turn other side to heat and cook for another 4-5 minutes. The inside should be thoroughly set and not runny. Open pan and carefully cut into two pieces.
- ◆ erve immediately on warmed plates. Garnish with parsley.

CHICKEN AND SPINACH CREPES

12 crepes

Crepes

1 cup flour
3 eggs
2 tablespoons butter, melted

1½ cups milk
¼ teaspoon salt

- ◆ Mix the ingredients together in a bowl.
- ◆ To make crepes use a six inch crepe pan or flat skillet.
- ◆ Using a ladle, pour a large spoonful of batter into the pan.
- ◆ Turn the crepe as soon as it puffs up. Remove from heat immediately.

Filling

1½ cups cooked chicken
1 pound cooked fresh spinach

2 cups roux

- ◆ Along the center of the crepe put 1 tablespoon each of chicken and spinach.
- ◆ Pour a small amount of roux over top. Roll up the crepe.
- ◆ Ham can be substituted for the chicken.

Roux

2 sticks butter
½ cup flour

2 cups milk

- ◆ Melt the butter in saucepan and slowly stir in the flour and then milk, until thickened.
- ◆ Place the crepes in a baking dish and pour the rest of the roux over the top.
- ◆ Bake in 350° oven for 20 minutes or until just slightly brown on top.
- ◆ 1 cup sharp cheddar cheese, Gruyere or Swiss cheese can be added to the roux.

CHEESE GRITS

Serves 8

1 cup uncooked grits
4 cups water
1 stick butter
½ pound sharp cheddar cheese

2 cloves garlic, minced
¼ teaspoon cayenne or dash of Tabasco

- ♦ In a saucepan boil four cups of water. Stir the grits into boiling water. Reduce the heat and cook about 5 minutes, until thickened.
- ♦ Add butter, cheese and garlic, stirring until cheese is melted.
- ♦ Pour into 2 quart casserole and bake 20 minutes at 350°.
- ♦ Serve hot
- ♦ For spicier grits add ½ teaspoon Tabasco sauce.

Brunch

Bloody Mary's/Mimosa's
Blueberry Muffins
Corned Beef Hash
Poached Eggs
Baked Grapefruit

LOUISE'S CORNED BEEF HASH

My former Mother-in-law made the best corned beef hash. This is a recreation from some of our Sunday mornings together. Serve with poached eggs and ketchup.

Serves 8

4-5 pounds cooked corned beef
8 potatoes, cooked and diced
1 cup onions, chopped

½ cup sour cream
½ cup ketchup
1 tablespoon chili powder

- ♦ Preheat the oven to 350°.
- ♦ Cut up the corned beef into bite size pieces.
- ♦ In a round casserole combine all the ingredients.
- ♦ Bake for 30-35 minutes until browned on top.

SANDWICHES

Tea Service – Mount Clare Mansion

Ladies' Tea

Watercress Sandwiches
Ron's Cinnamon Sticks
Miniature Crab Salad Sandwiches
Bread Loaf
Asparagus Sandwiches
Scones/Clotted Cream/Butter/Jams
Assorted Teas

MINIATURE CRAB SANDWICHES

Makes about 16 sandwiches

1 pound crab meat
¼ cup mayonnaise
¼ cup celery, diced
¼ cup red pepper, chopped

2 tablespoon onion, minced
¼ cup parsley, chopped
Thin sliced white bread

- ◆ Mix together all ingredients, except parsley and bread.
- ◆ Remove crusts from the bread.
- ◆ With a round cookie cutter cut rounds of thin white bread.
- ◆ Top rounds with crab meat and garnish with parsley

CRAB MEAT SALAD SANDWICHES

Makes 4 sandwiches

1 pound crab meat
¼ cup mayonnaise
¼ cup celery, diced

¼ cup red pepper, chopped
2 tablespoons onion, minced
2 Tbls. parsley, chopped

- ◆ Combine all ingredients.
- ◆ Spread on bread or rolls.

172

CRAB CAKE SANDWICH

Serves 4

4 crab cakes
4 sour dough rolls
Tartar sauce

Lemon slices

- Spread tartar sauce on each roll.
- Top with crab cake and squeeze of lemon juice.

FRIED OYSTER SANDWICH

Serves 4

12 fried oysters
Tartar sauce

Lemon juice
4 sour dough rolls

- Spread tartar sauce on rolls.
- Top with three oysters on each and lemon juice.

BREAD LOAF

This is quite a show stopper for a lady's tea.

Any number of salads or ingredients can be used on each layer. I remember my mother doing olives and cream cheese, watercress, sliced tomatoes, egg salad, salmon salad, tuna salad, and various other mixtures. Be inventive.

1 unsliced loaf of white bread
8 ounces cream cheese

3 cups chicken salad
Lettuce

- Take the crusts off the bread. Lengthwise slice bread into 4 layers.
- On three slices spread butter or mayonnaise and then chicken salad.
- Layer and top with last piece of bread.
- Cream the cheese and soften with a little milk. Spread the top and sides of the loaf with the cream cheese.
- Garnish with parsley and pimentos or sliced olives.

BACON, CHEESE AND TOMATO SANDWICHES

Serves 6

12 slices white bread
12 slices bacon, cooked

1 pound cheddar cheese
2 large tomatoes, sliced

- ◆ Preheat broiler.
- ◆ Place the bread slices on a cookie sheet. Cover each slice of bread with slices of cheese, then slice of tomato.
- ◆ Break each slice of bacon in two, and make cross on top of cheese. Place under broiler until cheese bubbles.

HOT TURKEY SANDWICH

Serves 4

8 slices French bread
1 red onion
16 slices smoked turkey

2 large tomatoes, sliced
½ pound Gruyere, sliced

- ◆ Preheat oven to 350°.
- ◆ Toast the French bread. Place the toast in one layer in a casserole.
- ◆ Layer with slices of tomato, onion and turkey.
- ◆ Top with Gruyere.
- ◆ Bake for 10 minutes, or put briefly under the broiler.

TURKEY SANDWICH

Makes 1 sandwich

2 slices turkey breast (smoked turkey is preferred)
1 slice Swiss cheese
2 slices bread

2 tablespoons mayonnaise
1 leaf lettuce
4 tbls. cranberry chutney

- ◆ Spread the bread with mayonnaise.
- ◆ Then layer with Swiss cheese, turkey, lettuce and chutney.
- ◆ Cut in half. Serve with extra chutney.

CHICKEN AND HAM TEA SANDWICHES

Makes 48 sandwiches

Chicken and Ham Filling

4 ounces skinless, boneless chicken breast, cooked and cooled
1 cup lean ham pieces
1 scallion, chopped
Dash of white pepper
½ teaspoon salt

½ cup half and half
1 cup Garlic and Herb Spreadable Cheese
12 slices thinly sliced bread

- Combine chicken, ham and scallion in a food processor, and process to a finely textured consistency. Add salt and pepper.
- Add half and half and process to a thick, spreadable consistency.

To Assemble

- Cut the crusts off the bread. Put a thin layer of the cheese spread on each slice.
- Spread the chicken and ham filling on half of the bread slices.
- Assemble the sandwiches and cut into quarters.

Courtesy of Deb Cathers, Wisteria Tea Cottage, Frederick, Maryland

CHICKEN MELT

Serves 4

2 large baked chicken breasts
¼ cup mayonnaise
¼ cup diced celery

2 tablespoons diced onion
2 tablespoons fresh basil

Place all the ingredients in a food processor until just blended together.

4 English muffins

½ cup cheddar cheese

- Spread the chicken mixture on halved English muffins. Sprinkle with grated cheddar cheese. Place under the broiler until cheese bubbles.

HAM SANDWICH

2 slices rye bread   2 slices Swiss cheese
2 slices Virginia ham   Dijon mustard

- Spread the bread with mustard, and then ham and cheese.
- Butter bread on outside of sandwich.
- Place in a skillet and brown each side.

HAM AND CHEESE SANDWICH

Makes 6 sandwiches

6 slices bread, toasted   6 eggs, separated
12 slices ham   ¼ cup mayonnaise
12 slices Swiss cheese   1 tablespoon Dijon mustard
Tabasco sauce

- Preheat the oven to 350°.
- In baking dish place the bread. Top each slice with ham and cheese.
- In a mixing bowl beat egg yolks, mayonnaise, mustard and Tabasco.
- Beat egg whites until peaks are formed and add to yolk mixture. Pour over bread.
- Bake about 20 minutes or until browned.

WATERCRESS SANDWICHES

Thin sliced bread   Mayonnaise (cream cheese can
Watercress without stem   also be used)

- Take the crusts off the bread and cut bread slices into round circles with a glass or round cutter. Spread the bread rounds with mayonnaise. Place a sprig of watercress on bread.

PEAR AND WALNUT TEA SANDWICHES

Makes 12 sandwiches

½ cup walnuts
4 ounces cream cheese
1 ripe pear
6 thin slices bread

¼ cup sugar
1 teaspoon cinnamon
¼ teaspoon fresh grated nutmeg

- Roast the walnuts in the oven at 400° for 10 minutes. Let cool and chop finely.
- Remove the skin and core from the pear. Cut the pear in half and make 36 very thin slices.
- Cut the crusts off the bread.
- Mix cinnamon and sugar together. Add nutmeg.
- Place cream cheese in a small bowl, and whip until soft and spreadable.
- Spread each slice of bread with a thin coating of the cream cheese.
- Sprinkle the cinnamon-sugar-nutmeg mixture over the cream cheese.
- Set aside 3 slices of the bread for the sandwich tops.
- On each of the remaining three slices, sprinkle about 1 tablespoon of the chopped walnuts on top of the cream cheese.
- Place six pear slices on top of the walnuts.
- Put the three tops on the sandwiches. Cut each sandwich into 4 triangles.

Courtesy of Deb Cathers, Wisteria Tea Cottage, Frederick, Maryland

CUCUMBER SANDWICHES

Thin white bread
Cucumber

Mayonnaise
Fresh dill

- Take the crusts off the bread and cut bread slices into round circles with a small glass or round cutter.
- Spread the bread rounds with mayonnaise.
- Put one slice cucumber on bread. Top with a sprig of fresh dill.

MUSHROOM SANDWICHES

½ pound mushrooms, chopped   Thin sliced white bread
8 ounces cream cheese

- ◆ Combine the cream cheese and mushrooms.
- ◆ Spread the mushroom mixture on the bread which has been cut into a triangular shape.
- ◆ These are also good put under the broiler until bubbling.

LILI'S ASPARAGUS ROLL-UPS

4 ounces blue cheese   16 stalks asparagus, blanched
8 ounces cream cheese   1 loaf thin sliced white bread
1 egg   1 stick butter
1 tablespoon mayonnaise

- ◆ Combine the cheeses, egg and mayonnaise until well blended.
- ◆ Take the crusts off the bread. Spread the cheese mixture on both sides of 16 slices of bread.
- ◆ Place each asparagus spear in the center of the bread.
- ◆ Roll up bread and cut into three pieces, using a toothpick for each section to keep in place.
- ◆ Melt the butter. Dip each roll into butter and place on an ungreased cookie sheet.
- ◆ Bake at 350° for 20 minutes. These can be frozen and reheated.

ASPARAGUS SANDWICHES

Makes 16 sandwiches

16 slices thin white bread   Mayonnaise
16 spears asparagus   Pimento strips

- ◆ In a skillet boil enough water to cover the asparagus spears. When boiling put in spears and cook for 4 minutes. Remove and drain.
- ◆ Take the crusts off the bread. Spread mayonnaise on bread.
- ◆ Place asparagus spear in center of the bread. Roll up bread.
- ◆ Serve on a platter. Garnish with pimento strips

CHICKEN SALAD SANDWICHES

Hough Bakery in Cleveland always had the best chicken salad sandwiches. The salad was very fine and rich. Ham can be substituted for the chicken.

Thin sliced bread

Chicken salad

2 chicken breasts, cooked
½ cup mayonnaise
1 small stalk celery
2 tablespoons onion

1 tablespoon fresh basil
Salt and pepper to taste
Butter

- Place all the ingredients in a food processor. Blend until just mixed together, but not mushy.
- Take the crusts off the bread.
- Spread each bread slice with just a little butter and chicken salad.
- Roll up bread. Or top with another slice of bread and cut in half across diagonal.

HOT STEAK SANDWICH

Serves 4

1 pound steak, grilled
Olive oil
1 large onion

½ pound Gruyere
8 slices French Bread

- Slice the steak very thin.
- Saute the onions in a skillet with olive oil until tender. Add steak until warmed.
- Layer the steak and onions on the French bread.
- Top with Gruyere.
- Place under broiler until the cheese is just browned.
- Swiss or Monterey jack cheese can be substituted for the Gruyere.
- This can also be served as an hors d'oeuvre.

CHUTNEYS, JAMS
AND SAUCES

Hard Times – Tilghman, Maryland

FAITH'S CRANBERRY CHUTNEY

Faith is our wonderful neighbor on Nantucket Island. Several years ago I spent the winter there, and while doing so she shared this recipe with me. I usually triple the recipe so that the jars can be given as presents at Christmas and throughout the year.

Cranberries are not native to the Chesapeake Bay region, but this cranberry chutney is so good with turkey, chicken or pork.

4 cups cranberries
½ cup vinegar
1 cup sugar
2 cups water
1 good size red onion

1 cup walnuts
1 cup currants or raisins
¼ cup fresh ginger, grated
½ teaspoon cloves
½ teaspoon cayenne

- ◆ In a large pot boil the cranberries, vinegar, sugar and water until the mixture thickens.
- ◆ Stir in the walnuts, currants and spices.
- ◆ Sterilize the jars in boiling water.
- ◆ Pour the chutney into jars and cover with parafin.

PEACH CHUTNEY

12 large peaches, peeled, pitted and cut into small pieces
1 cup chopped red onion
1 cup raisins

2 cups white wine vinegar
3 cups sugar
4 cloves garlic, crushed
1 small jar candied ginger

- ◆ In a large pan bring the vinegar and sugar to a boil.
- ◆ Add the peaches, onion, raisins, garlic and ginger.
- ◆ Cook two hours, occasionally stirring.
- ◆ Sterilize the jars in boiling water.
- ◆ Pour the chutney into the jars and seal with parafin.

APPLE CHUTNEY

8 cups apples, peeled and chopped
4½ cups sugar
2 cups raisins
1 cup walnuts or pecans

1 cup onions, chopped
½ cup cider vinegar
Peel of 2 lemons, chopped
½ teaspoon cloves
1 Tbls. freshly grated ginger

- ◆ Combine all the ingredients in a saucepan and bring to boil.
- ◆ Simmer until the apples are tender and the syrup has thickened.
- ◆ Sterilize the jars and ladle chutney into jars. Seal and store.

BRANDIED PEACHES

4 pounds peaches
2 cups sugar

1 cup brandy

- ◆ Put the peaches in a boiling pot of water (to cover peaches) and then cook until skins are easily removed, about 5 minutes. Remove the pits and cut into quarters. Place the peaches into a pot of boiling water again and bring to a boil. Cook until the peaches are tender.
- ◆ Pack the peaches in sterilized jars.
- ◆ Combine the brandy and sugar. Pour over the peaches and seal.
- ◆ This is delicious served over vanilla ice cream.

CORN RELISH

Corn relish is often served with roasted or fried oysters.

12 ears corn
3 green peppers
1 head cabbage
3 red peppers
1 quart cider vinegar
4 onions

1 bunch celery
2 teaspoons mustard seed
2 teaspoons celery seed
2 cups sugar
2 tablespoons salt
¼ teaspoon cayenne

- ◆ Cut the corn kernels from the cob.
- ◆ Chop the peppers, celery, onions and cabbage into small pieces.
- ◆ Put all ingredients in a large pot and stir. Bring to a boil. Simmer for 30 minutes.
- ◆ Spoon into sterilized jars and seal.

WATERMELON PICKLE

This is a delicious way to use watermelon rind. It will keep all winter.

1 pound watermelon rind, cut into small pieces
3 cinnamon sticks
8 cloves
Rind of 1 orange

Rind of 1 lemon
1 tablespoon fresh ginger
1 cup water
2 cups sugar
1 cup vinegar

- Boil watermelon rind in water for about 10 minutes. Drain.
- Make a spice bag out of cheesecloth with the cinnamon sticks, cloves, rinds and ginger.
- Place the bag in a pan with the water, sugar and vinegar. Boil until a thick sauce forms.
- Add the rind and again bring to a boil.
- Place the watermelon rind in sterilized jars and cover with liquid. Seal with parafin.

EASY HOLLANDAISE

1 stick butter
3 egg yolks

Juice of ½ lemon

- Melt butter in a small saucepan.
- Into food processor put egg yolks. Blend until smooth.
- Slowly pour butter into processor while blending.
- Add lemon juice.
- Serve with broccoli, fish, or on Eggs Benedict.

PESTO

1 large bunch basil leaves
½ cup parmesan cheese
¼ cup pine nuts

2 cloves garlic
¼ cup olive oil

- Combine all the ingredients in a food processor until the basil is very finely chopped.
- Serve over pasta, chicken, tomatoes, or other dishes.

HORSERADISH SAUCE

Serve with lamb, beef or pork roasts.

1 cup sour cream   ½ cup horseradish
½ cup whipped cream

- ♦ Combine the ingredients in a bowl.

RAISIN SAUCE FOR HAM

1 cup raisins   ¼ teaspoon dry mustard
1¾ cups water   ¼ teaspoon ground cloves
¼ cup brown sugar   ¼ teaspoon salt
1½ tablespoons cornstarch   1 tablespoon butter
¼ teaspoon cinnamon   1 tablespoon vinegar

- ♦ Boil raisins in water for 5 minutes.
- ♦ Combine the dry ingredients in a bowl. Add to raisin mixture.
- ♦ Cook 15 minutes. Stir in butter and vinegar.
- ♦ Serve in a bowl with baked ham.

OUR FAVORITE SALAD DRESSING

¼ cup honey   ¼ cup olive oil
¼ cup balsamic vinegar   1 tablespoon Dijon mustard

- ♦ Put the ingredients in a jar. Shake well.
- ♦ Store in the refrigerator. Use as needed.

HERB DRESSING

1 cup olive oil   2 cloves garlic
¼ cup tarragon vinegar   2 Tbls. fresh parsley
1 teaspoon Dijon mustard   1 teaspoon ground pepper
¼ cup fresh basil

- ♦ Combine all the ingredients in a food processor.
- ♦ Serve over a green salad.

DESSERTS

The early desserts served in this region included peaches in brandy, plum pudding, tarts, ice cream, figs, almonds and raisins. For dinner parties hostesses would have an elaborate table set only for the desserts.

Mount Clare Dining Room at Christmas

FUDGE

Fudge was invented in Baltimore in 1886. The recipe was taken to Vassar College by Emelyn Hartridge, class of 1892.

2 cups sugar
1 tablespoon butter
1 cup cream

8 ounces Baker's Premium No.1 unsweetened chocolate

- ♦ In a pan very slowly melt the chocolate with the cream and sugar, stirring constantly.
- ♦ When this begins to boil add butter.
- ♦ Remove from heat and beat until cool.
- ♦ Pour into buttered tins.
- ♦ Refrigerate and then cut into diamond-shaped pieces.

MRS. CARROLL'S MACAROONS

Macaroons have been around for a long time and were served in early colonial days. This recipe comes from Mrs. Charles Carroll of Mount Clare Mansion in Baltimore.

3 cups almonds, blanched
1 teaspoon rose water

4 egg whites
2 cups sugar

- ♦ Place almonds and rose water in blender until nuts are very fine.
- ♦ Beat egg whites until frothy.
- ♦ Gradually add sugar and beat until stiff.
- ♦ Drop by teaspoonful on baking pans covered with brown paper.
- ♦ Bake at 300° for 25 minutes.
- ♦ Makes approximately 8 dozen cookies.

Courtesy of "Some of Mrs. Carroll's Favorite Recipes"

LADY BALTIMORE CAKE

There are number of different versions of Lady Baltimore Cake. Cakes were an important part of the dessert table. Imperial and Queen Cakes had much richer ingredients than Lady Cakes. Lady Cakes were baked in the 1800's and similar to a rich pound cake. The Lady Baltimore Cake was noted for its sweet walnut filling.

1 cup butter	3 cups flour
2 cups sugar	3 teaspoons baking powder
6 egg whites	½ teaspoon salt
1 cup milk	1 teaspoon vanilla

- ◆ Cream butter and sugar together.
- ◆ Add all other ingredients except egg whites.
- ◆ Beat egg whites until stiff. Fold egg whites into batter.
- ◆ Pour into 3 buttered 9" cake pans.
- ◆ Bake in 350° oven for 25 minutes. Remove from oven and let cool.

Filling and Frosting

1½ cups sugar	1 cup walnuts
½ teaspoon cream of tartar	6 fresh figs, finely chopped
¼ teaspoon salt	1 teaspoon almond extract
1 teaspoon vanilla	2 egg whites
½ cup chopped raisins	½ cup water

- ◆ In a double boiler combine the egg whites, sugar, salt, water and cream of tartar. Beat until stiff.
- ◆ Remove from heat and add vanilla. Divide in half.
- ◆ In another bowl beat ½ frosting with raisins, nuts, figs and almond extract.
- ◆ Pour this filling on each layer and ice the cake with the other half.

HOWARD MOOSE'S RAW APPLE CAKE

1 cup Wesson oil
2 cups sugar
2 eggs
1 cup black walnuts
1 cup raisins
3 cups flour

1 teaspoon salt
1 teaspoon soda
3 cups raw (sour apples)
2 tablespoons molasses
1 teaspoon apple pie spices

♦ Cream oil and sugar. Add eggs and beat well. Mix in dry ingredients.
♦ Add floured walnuts and raisins, then raw apples sliced very thin.
♦ Bake in sheet pan or greased and floured tube pan at 325° for 45 minutes.

Icing

1 cup brown sugar
½ cup sweet condensed milk

1 stick butter
1 teaspoon vanilla

♦ Combine all in the ingredients in a saucepan and bring the mixture to a boil. Cook two minutes and then pour over cake.

Now Let Us Praise Fried Pies

BAKED PEARS

Serves 6

4 macaroons
2 pounds ripe pears
¼ cup white wine

¼ cup apricot jam
¼ cup butter, melted

♦ Peel, core and slice the pears lengthwise and arrange in a buttered baking dish.
♦ Combine the wine and jam, and pour over the pears.
♦ Crush macaroons in food processor and sprinkle over pears. Pour butter over mixture
♦ Bake at 400° for 25 minutes. Serve with vanilla ice cream.

BAKED APPLES

Serves 6

6 apples cored   ¼ cup brown sugar
1 cup raisins   6 tablespoons butter, melted
1 tablespoon cinnamon

- ◆ Preheat the oven to 350°.
- ◆ Mix together the raisins, cinnamon, and sugar.
- ◆ Stuff each apple with the mixture.
- ◆ Place the apples in a baking dish. Pour the butter over the apples. Bake for 30 minutes.
- ◆ Serve with vanilla or butter pecan ice cream, or whipped cream.
- ◆ Cranberries can be substituted for the raisins.
- ◆ ½ cup pecans or walnuts can also be added.

INDIAN PUDDING

Ever since we were children we loved Indian pudding. Coming home from evening walks with my paternal grandmother she would serve this or blueberries with ice cream. What a way to have sweet dreams.

2 cups milk   ½ stick butter, melted
½ cup sugar   1 teaspoon cinnamon
½ cup molasses   ¼ teaspoon grated nutmeg
½ cup cornmeal   ¼ teaspoon mace

- ◆ Preheat the oven to 350°.
- ◆ Boil the milk in a saucepan and stir in the sugar, molasses and cornmeal until thickened.
- ◆ In a bowl beat together the eggs and add the spices and butter. Beat in the cornmeal mix.
- ◆ Pour the batter into an 8" round ovenproof bowl. Bake for 35 minutes. Serve with vanilla ice cream.

STRAWBERRY MOUSSE

Serves 6

1 envelope unflavored gelatin	2 tablespoons rum
2 tablespoons boiling water	½ cup sugar
Juice of 1 lemon	2 egg yolks
1 quart strawberries	2 cups whipping cream

- ◆ Combine gelatin and water in a small saucepan. Stir in lemon juice.
- ◆ Then add strawberries (save 6 for garnish) and rum. Bring to a boil. Cool to room temperature.
- ◆ Beat together egg yolks and sugar in a saucepan, and cook until thickened over low heat. Let cool.
- ◆ Fold the berries into the egg and sugar mixture.
- ◆ Whip the cream until soft peaks are formed and fold into strawberry mixture.
- ◆ Serve individually in wine goblets or glass bowls.
- ◆ Garnish with remaining strawberries.
- ◆ Peaches, raspberries, blackberries or other fruit can be substituted for the strawberries.

STRAWBERRY SHORTCAKE

This is an easy recipe using store bought pound cake. Sweet biscuits can be substituted for the pound cake.

1 pound cake	1 pint whipping cream
1 quart strawberries	¼ cup sugar

- ◆ Whip the cream until stiff. Fold in the sugar.
- ◆ Frost the cake with the whipping cream.
- ◆ Decorate the cake with the strawberries.

RASPBERRY PARFAIT

4 servings

1 pint fresh raspberries
1 cup coconut macaroon cookies
1 tablespoon butter, melted
½ teaspoon almond extract

Vanilla ice cream
Raspberry sherbet
Whipped cream

- Crumble the macaroons in a bowl, and add almond extract and melted butter.
- In parfait glasses alternate layers of the macaroon mixture, ice creams and berries.
- Top with a berry and whipped cream.

RASPBERRY-LEMON PIE

1 pint raspberries
1 can condensed sweetened milk
¼ cup lemon juice

3 egg yolks
Graham cracker pie crust

- Beat together milk and egg yolks in a bowl. Add lemon juice.
- Pour into a pie crust. Refrigerate.
- Just before serving top with raspberries.
- Key lime juice can be substituted for the lemon juice.

LEMON SOUFFLE

2 3 ounce packages lemon flavored gelatin
2 cups boiling water
8 ounces cream cheese
¼ cup sugar

¼ cup cold water
½ cup lemon juice
2 cups whipping cream
1 quart strawberries

- Dissolve gelatin in boiling water.
- Combine cream cheese and sugar in a bowl.
- Add gelatin, cold water and lemon juice, blending well.
- Chill until thickened. Fold in whipped cream
- Pour into a 1 quart souffle dish. Chill until firm
- Serve with strawberries and whipped cream

Easter Dinner

Grilled leg of Lamb
Mint Sauce
Parsley Red Potatoes
Asparagus with Sesame Seeds
Rolls/Butter
Lime Mousse

LIME MOUSSE

This colorful dessert should be served in the early spring when the strawberries are at their best.

Serves 8

8 egg yolks
1 cup sugar
1 cup fresh lime juice
½ teaspoon salt

3 cups heavy cream
2 teaspoons grated lime peel
1 quart strawberries

- ◆ Beat the egg yolks in a double boiler pan. Then add sugar lime juice and salt. Cook until the sauce thickens. Cool.
- ◆ In a bowl beat the cream until stiff. Fold in the cooled sauce and lime peel.
- ◆ Place in a round mold that has been rinsed in cool water and chilled.
- ◆ Chill mold until ready to serve.
- ◆ Unmold onto a serving plate. In the center of the mold place the strawberries. Decorate with thin lime slices.

CORNFLAKE RING

2 cups brown sugar
2 sticks butter
½ cup chopped pecans

½ package cornflakes
1 teaspoon vanilla
Ice cream

- ◆ Boil brown sugar and butter until a ball forms when placed in cold water.
- ◆ Combine the rest of the ingredients. Pack into a buttered ring mold.
- ◆ Refrigerate.
- ◆ Serve with your favorite flavor of ice cream in the center.

MISS LORETTA'S SWEET POTATO PIE

Loretta Larrimore was raised in Easton and married the captain of the skipjack *Lady Katie*. She has prepared many a meal for the *Lady Katie*, her family and friends.

This pie just melts in your mouth, as does her crab imperial.

2 cups sweet potato
1½ cups sugar
1½ cups half and half
½ stick butter
3 eggs beaten
Pinch of salt

1 teaspoon vanilla
1 teaspoon baking powder
1 teaspoon lemon juice
1 9 inch pie crust
Nutmeg

- Peel and boil the sweet potatoes until tender. Mash the sweet potatoes.
- Blend all the ingredients together, except for the nutmeg.
- Pour into a pie crust.
- Bake 35 minutes at 325°.
- Garnish with freshly grated nutmeg.

SWEET POTATO PECAN PIE

1 cup cooked sweet potato
4 eggs
¼ cup sugar
½ cup pecans
½ cup milk

½ cup orange juice
1 teaspoon vanilla
9 inch pie crust
½ pint whipping cream
1 teaspoon nutmeg

- Beat together the sweet potato, eggs, sugar, pecans, milk, orange juice and vanilla..
- Pour the sweet potato mixture into the crust.
- Bake at 375° for 40 minutes.
- Serve with whipped cream mixed with nutmeg.

POT DE CRÈME

Serves 4

4 oz. dark chocolate
¼ cup sugar
½ cup whipping cream

2 egg yolks
½ teaspoon vanilla

- ◆ In saucepan place chocolate, sugar and cream. Over low heat stir ingredients together until chocolate is melted.
- ◆ Remove from heat and add two beaten egg yolks and vanilla. Stir until smooth.
- ◆ Pour into individual pot de crème (demitasse cups may be substituted). Refrigerate.
- ◆ Before serving whip ½ cup whipping cream and garnish each cup.

LUCINDA'S RED, WHITE AND BLUE PIE

This is a perfect Fourth of July dessert, engineered by my daughter.

Pastry

1 stick butter
1¼ cups flour

¼ cup water

- ◆ Blend all three ingredients in food processor until a ball is formed.
- ◆ Place pastry on floured board and roll into a round shape for 9" pie plate. Place in pie plate.
- ◆ Bake in 400° oven for 10 minutes, or edges are browned.

Filling

1 cup whipping cream
¼ cup sugar

1 pint blueberries
1 pint strawberries

- ◆ Whip the cream until peaks are formed. Beat in sugar.
- ◆ After the pie crust is cooled spread whipped cream in crust.
- ◆ With your eye divide pie into 4 portions.
- ◆ Place a few of the strawberries in one section and its opposite section. Do the same with the blueberries.

194

PUMPKIN CHEESECAKE

Crust

3 cups ginger snaps
½ cup sugar

½ cup butter, melted

♦ Combine the ingredients and press into 2 pie plates.

Filling

16 ounces cream cheese
1 cup light cream
2 cups pumpkin
¾ cup sugar
4 egg yolks
4 egg whites, beaten until stiff

3 tablespoons flour
1 teaspoon vanilla
1 teaspoon cinnamon
½ teaspoon ginger
½ teaspoon nutmeg
¼ teaspoon salt

♦ Combine all ingredients except egg whites. Fold in egg whites.
♦ Pour filling into 2 crusts. Bake 325° for one hour.

MINCEMEAT CHEESECAKE

Crust

1½ cups graham cracker crumbs
¼ cup butter, melted

¼ cup sugar

♦ Combine all ingredients and press into pie shell.

Filling

1 large jar mincemeat
¼ cup bourbon or dark rum
16 ounces cream cheese
½ cup sugar

2 eggs
1 tablespoon grated lemon peel
½ teaspoon vanilla
1 tablespoon lemon juice

♦ Beat together cream cheese, sugar, lemon juice, lemon peel, vanilla and eggs.
♦ Mix bourbon with mincemeat.
♦ Pour mincemeat into pie crust and top with cream cheese mix.
♦ Bake 35 minutes at 375°. Refrigerate until served.

GINGERBREAD

2 cups flour
1½ teaspoons baking soda
2 teaspoons ginger
1 teaspoon cinnamon
1 cup molasses

½ cup butter
1 cup brown sugar
1 egg
½ cup milk

- Preheat oven to 350°
- Cream together butter and sugar, and then add molasses.
- Add flour, baking soda, ginger, cinnamon, egg and milk. Beat thoroughly.
- Pour into a 9" square baking dish. Bake for 30 –35 minutes.
- Serve with hard sauce.
- For a variation ½ cup applesauce can be added.

CANTALOUPE WITH SHERBET

This is also very good using honeydew melons.

Serves 4

1 cantaloupe
1 pint mint sherbet

Fresh mint leaves

- Cut the cantaloupe into four slices. Top each with a scoop of mint sherbet ice cream. Decorate with fresh mint.

BROWNIES FOR SKINNY PEOPLE

2 sticks butter
4 ounces unsweetened chocolate
4 eggs

2 cups sugar
1 cup flour
1 teaspoon vanilla

- Melt the chocolate and butter in a saucepan over low heat.
- Stir in sugar, eggs, flour and vanilla.
- ½ cup pecans or walnuts can also be added.
- Bake in an 8 inch square pan at 350° for 30 minutes.

ELIZABETH'S BROWNIES

6 ounces unsalted butter
4 squares baker's unsweetened chocolate
1½ cups sugar
¼ cup cocoa

1½ teaspoons vanilla
4 eggs
¾ cup all purpose flour
½ teaspoon baking powder
1 teaspoon salt

- Preheat oven to 350°.
- Grease an 8" non-stick square pan.
- In a 1½ quart microwaveable bowl melt the chocolate and butter on high about 2 minutes or until the chocolate is almost melted, and stir to continue melting.
- Meanwhile measure all the dry ingredients in a small bowl and whisk together to incorporate the baking powder to the flour.
- Add the sugar, cocoa and vanilla and stir till the sugar is well blended. Add the eggs and stir well.
- Add the dry ingredients, blending in all ingredients.
- Bake about 25 minutes or till a toothpick comes out a very moist crumble.

Courtesy of Elizabeth A. French, Elizabeth's Distinctive Confections, Severna Park, Maryland

CHIP BARS

1 stick butter
1½ cups graham cracker crumbs
1 can sweetened condensed milk
1 cup butterscotch chips

1 cup chocolate chips
1 cup pecans, chopped
1¼ cups coconut

- Preheat the oven to 350°.
- Melt the butter in a 9" x 13" baking pan in the oven.
- Sprinkle the graham cracker crumbs over the butter and then pour milk over this.
- Top with the remaining ingredients.
- Bake 25 minutes.

GEORGE'S BOURBON BALLS

Our lady friends love these as gifts at Christmas.

2 Tbls. unsweetened cocoa
¾ cup powdered sugar
¼ teaspoon edible gold powder
2 cups vanilla wafer crumbs

½ cup finely chopped pecans
¼ cup bourbon
2 tablespoons honey

- ◆ Combine cocoa, sugar, gold powder and honey.
- ◆ Roast the pecans in the oven.
- ◆ Combine bourbon, honey, pecans and crumbs. Shape into balls.
- ◆ Roll balls in gold powder, cocoa and sugar mixture.
- ◆ Gingersnaps can be substituted for the vanilla wafers.

THE BEST CARROT CAKE

We have tried many times to make this cake with butter. Vegetable oil works best for a good consistency.

1½ cups vegetable oil
2 cups sugar
4 eggs
1 cups flour
2 teaspoons baking powder

½ teaspoon salt
1 tablespoon cinnamon
2 teaspoons vanilla
3 cups grated carrots (do in food processor)

- ◆ Combine the oil, sugar and eggs in a large mixing bowl.
- ◆ Add flour, baking powder, salt, cinnamon, vanilla and last the carrots.
- ◆ Bake in 2 9 inch cake pans at 325° for 45 minutes.
- ◆ Remove from oven and cool.

Cream Cheese Frosting:

1 stick butter
1 8 ounce package cream cheese

1 package confectioners' sugar
2 teaspoons vanilla

- ◆ Beat all ingredients in mixing bowl.
- ◆ Frost the cake with cream cheese frosting.

APPLE PIE

Crust

1 stick butter
1¼ cups flour
¼ cup water

1 tablespoon sugar
3 Tbls. cream cheese

- In food processor blend butter, sugar, cream cheese and flour. Add only enough water to form ball.
- Place on floured cutting board and roll into shape of pie dish.

Filling

4 large apples, cored, leaving skins on and sliced thinly
¼ cup sugar
¼ cup brown sugar

¼ cup flour
1 teaspoon cinnamon
½ stick butter
½ teaspoon ground ginger

- Line pie crust with apples, overlapping in a circle.
- In small bowl mix together sugars, flour, cinnamon and butter. Pour over apples.
- Bake in 350° oven for ½ hour or until crust is browned.
- Serve warm with vanilla or butter pecan ice cream.
- To vary the recipe, add ½ cup raisins, pecans, walnuts, or cranberries.

HOT FRUIT COMPOTE

During the winter canned fruit can be substituted for fresh fruit.

Serves 6-8

½ stick butter
1 cup brown sugar
1 teaspoon cinnamon
1 teaspoon ginger

2 cups peeled and sliced peaches
2 cups peeled and sliced pears
1 pint strawberries
1 pint blueberries

- Preheat oven to 350°
- Combine all ingredients in a baking dish.
- Bake for 30 minutes. Serve hot.

Southern Dinner

Ham
Grits
Biscuits
Watercress Salad
Utterly Deadly Southern Pecan Pie

AUNT PHYL'S UTTERLY DEADLY SOUTHERN PECAN PIE

Every Thanksgiving and Christmas we have this. Aunt Phyl was the most theatrical lady New Castle could ever know – a true "Auntie Mame". We loved her in her various flowing gowns, pulled back and up hairdos, and a time filled with laughter.

4 eggs, beaten	4 tablespoons butter
1½ cups pecans	1 teaspoon vanilla
1 cup sugar	1 9 inch pie crust
1½ cups cane sugar	

- Boil sugars together in a saucepan. Add butter, eggs, vanilla and pecans.
- Pour into an unbaked pie shell.
- Bake 350° for 45 minutes.

BLUEBERRY DELIGHT

Serves 4

1 pint blueberries, washed	1 cup brown sugar
1 cup sour cream	

- Put blueberries in individual bowls.
- Allow guests to put desired amount of sour cream and brown sugar on blueberries.

RUTHIE'S BLUEBERRY PIE

Crust

½ cup oil
2 tablespoons milk
1½ cups flour

½ teaspoon salt
1½ teaspoons sugar

+ Combine ingredients in bowl, kneading well with hands.
+ Press into pie plate for crust.

Filling

2 pints blueberries
1 cup sugar

1 tablespoon cornstarch
1½ tablespoons lemon juice

+ Combine ingredients and pour into pie shell.

Topping

½ stick butter
½ cup flour

½ cup sugar
1 teaspoon cinnamon

+ Combine these last ingredients and pour over blueberry mix.
+ Bake pie 10 minutes in 425° oven and then for 35 minutes at 350°.

FROZEN GRAPES

Serves 6

2 pounds grapes
1 cup brown sugar

1 cup sour cream

+ Take stems off grapes, and place grapes in plastic bag in freezer.
+ Freeze one hour or until solid. Do not take out until just before serving.
+ Put grapes into individual bowls and serve with sour cream and brown sugar.

KEY LIME PIE

Though key limes do not come from the Chesapeake Bay region, key lime pie is still a refreshing way to finish off a good seafood dinner. This is also a very easy recipe. Fresh limes or lemons can be substituted for key limes.

9" pie crust
¼ cup key lime juice

1 can condensed sweetened milk
3 eggs

- Bake pie crust in 400° oven for 10 minutes or until slightly browned.

Filling

- In small mixing bowl separate egg whites from egg yolks. Beat egg whites until firm.
- Beat egg yolks in a separate bowl and add condensed milk and key lime juice.
- Pour key lime mixture into cooled pie crust. Top with beaten egg whites.
- Place under broiler for about 10 seconds (keep an eye on this).
- Store in refrigerator until used. Best served same day as made, though it can be frozen.

PEANUT LACE COOKIES

1 cup flour
1 cup chopped peanuts
½ cup karo syrup

½ cup butter
½ cup brown sugar
1 teaspoon vanilla

- Preheat oven to 325°.
- In a saucepan combine the syrup, butter, and brown sugar, stirring until it comes to a boil. Remove from the heat.
- Mix together the peanuts and flour and add to the syrup mixture.
- Stir in the vanilla.
- Drop by the teaspoonful on an ungreased cookie sheet, leaving room for the cookie to spread.
- Bake 8-10 minutes, or until just browned.
- Let cool 3-5 minutes and remove to wire rack.
- These are delicious with vanilla ice cream.

PEANUT BUTTER COOKIES

These are my father's favorite cookies

1 cup butter
½ teaspoon salt
1 cup peanut butter
1 cup sugar
1 cup firmly packed brown sugar

2 eggs
1 tablespoon milk
2 cups flour
1 teaspoon baking soda

- ◆ Preheat oven to 350°.
- ◆ Mix butter, salt and peanut butter.
- ◆ Add both sugars, beating until creamy.
- ◆ Add eggs and milk, then flour and soda.
- ◆ Drop by teaspoons on lightly greased cookie sheet.
- ◆ Bake about 10 minutes.

THE VERY BEST CHOCOLATE CHIP COOKIES

2 cups butter
2 cups brown sugar
2 cups white sugar
4 eggs
4 cups flour
2 teaspoons vanilla
5 cups old-fashioned oats

1 teaspoon salt
2 teaspoons baking powder
2 teaspoons baking soda
2 packages chocolate chips
1 8 ounce Hershey Bar grated
3 cups chopped nuts, toasted

- ◆ Preheat oven to 375°.
- ◆ Cream together the butter and sugars, add eggs and milk.
- ◆ Then mix in flour, oatmeal, salt, baking powder and soda.
- ◆ Add chocolate chips, chocolate and nuts.
- ◆ Roll dough into balls
- ◆ place on cookie sheet and bake for 6 minutes.
- ◆ Makes about 9 dozen cookies.

GINGER SNAPS

Makes about six dozen cookies.

1½ sticks butter
1 cup sugar
2 cups flour
1 egg
¼ cup molasses

2 teaspoons baking soda
1 teaspoon powdered cinnamon
1 teaspoon powdered cloves
1 teaspoon ginger
Sugar

- In a bowl cream the butter and add sugar, egg, molasses and beat well.
- Add dry ingredients.
- Refrigerate 2 hours.
- Roll into marble size balls and then in sugar.
- Baked on greased cookie sheet for 8-10 minutes at 350°.

Now Let Us Praise Fried Pies

SNOWBALLS

As a child this was one of our favorite desserts along with Tiger Dunlap Delight. Delicious and easy. Kids love it.

William Blake, while visiting Maryland in 1744, first records ice cream as being served with strawberries at a dinner given by Gov. Thomas Bladen (1742-47) in Annapolis.

In 1851 Jacob Fussel, who sold milk in Baltimore, used surplus cream to make into ice cream and became the first major ice cream producer in Baltimore. His market later expanded into Washington, Boston, New York, Cincinnati, Chicago and as far west as St. Louis.

Vanilla ice cream
Coconut

Chocolate sauce
Caramel sauce

- Soften ice cream just slightly. Using an ice cream scooper make into balls.
- Roll the balls in coconut.
- Top with one of the sauces, or both.

TIGER DUNLAP DELIGHT

When we lived in Birmingham, Michigan in the late 1950s my parents would take us once or twice a year up to Stratford, Ontario. We would stay at a wonderful place called the Tiger Dunlap Inn. Our favorite dessert was Tiger Dunlap Delight. This is my recreation of that wonderful dessert.

Pound cake
Vanilla ice cream
Butterscotch sauce

Whipped cream
Cherries

- On a slice of pound cake put one large scoop of ice cream.
- Top with hot butterscotch sauce, whipped cream and cherries.

MOCHA ANGEL FOOD CAKE

My mother always serves this cake for our birthdays

Angel food cake

Frosting

1 box confectioners sugar
1 stick butter, softened
1 teaspoon vanilla

½ cup coffee
½ cup cocoa

- Beat together sugar, butter, vanilla, chocolate and coffee.
- Spread on top of cake and let run down sides.

SQUASH PUDDING

1 package frozen squash
½ cup chopped walnuts
¼ pound marshmallows

¼ cup dark brown sugar
½ cup raisins
Whipping cream

- Heat in a saucepan all ingredients except marshmallows and cream.
- Pour into baking dish and place marshmallows on top.
- Put under broiler until browned.
- Serve with whipped cream.

SALLIE'S SWEET POTATO PUDDING

4 eggs
2 cups sugar
2 cups sweet potatoes or yams
2 cups scalded milk

¼ pound butter, melted
1 tablespoon cornstarch
1 tablespoon water
2 teaspoons ginger

- Preheat oven to 350°.
- Grate the sweet potatoes.
- Dissolve the cornstarch in the water.
- Beat eggs until light. Add sugar and sweet potatoes, then milk and butter, cornstarch and ginger. Cook gently until thickened.
- Place in buttered baking dish and bake 20 minutes.
- Serve with whipped cream or vanilla ice cream.

Now Let Us Praise Fried Pies

MOTHER'S SWEET POTATO CUSTARD

2 large sweet potatoes, not yams
1 cup milk
1 cup sugar
2 eggs

1 teaspoon nutmeg
1 teaspoon cinnamon
½ teaspoon ginger
1 9 inch pie crust

- Preheat to 425°.
- Boil, peel and mash potatoes. Add other ingredients and mix well.
- Pour into pie crust. Bake 40-50 minutes or until a knife inserted in the center comes out clean.

Now Let Us Praise Fried Pies

LOU'S RITZ PIE

3 egg whites, beaten stiffly
1 cup chopped pecans
1 teaspoon vanilla or rum

1 cup sugar
20 crumbled Ritz crackers

- ◆ Combine all ingredients in a bowl and put in pie plate.
- ◆ Bake at 325° for 30 minutes.
- ◆ Chill overnight.

PRUNE WHIP WITH CUSTARD SAUCE

1 cup stewed prunes
4 egg whites
½ cup sugar

½ teaspoon lemon juice
Pinch of salt

- ◆ Strain prunes into a saucepan and add sugar. Cook 5 minutes.
- ◆ Chill. Add lemon juice and salt.
- ◆ Beat egg whites until stiff. Fold into the prune mixture. Chill.

Custard Sauce

3 egg yolks
¼ cup sugar
2 cups scalded milk

1 tablespoon vanilla, rum or brandy

- ◆ Cook all the ingredients in a saucepan over low heat until thickened.
- ◆ Serve over the prune whip.

AUNT KIM'S FUDGE SAUCE

1 cup sugar
½ cup milk
½ cup cocoa

½ stick butter
1 teaspoon vanilla

- ◆ Combine ingredients in a saucepan until thick. Add vanilla.
- ◆ Delicious served hot over ice cream or brownies.
- ◆ To make fudge use this recipe, but add only ½ cup milk. Cook until the soft ball stage. Place in a sinkful of cold water. When thickened pour into a buttered dish. Cool. Cut in 1 inch wedges.

EASY APPLESAUCE CAKE

1 package apple spice cake mix   1 cup applesauce

♦ Prepare mix as directed. Add applesauce. Cook as directed.

Frosting

2 cups confectioner's sugar   3 tablespoons milk
¼ cup butter   1 teaspoon vanilla

♦ Cream butter and add confectioner's sugar, vanilla and milk. Beat until smooth. Spread over cake.
♦ Cream cheese frosting can be substituted – see carrot cake

Now Let Us Praise Fried Pies

APPLESAUCE CAKE

2 cups flour   ½ cup butter
1 teaspoon soda   1 cup sugar
¼ teaspoon salt   1 egg
1 teaspoon cinnamon   1 cup chopped nuts
1 teaspoon cloves   1 cup raisins
1 teaspoon nutmeg   1 cup applesauce

♦ Preheat oven to 350°.
♦ Cream butter and add sugar, beating well together. Add egg, nuts and raisins.
♦ Add dry ingredients alternately with applesauce until smooth.
♦ Pour into greased loaf pan. Bake for 1 hour and 15 minutes.

Frosting (Cream cheese frosting can be substituted – see carrot cake)

2 cups confectioner's sugar   3 tablespoons milk
¼ cup butter   1 teaspoon vanilla

♦ Cream butter and add confectioner's sugar, vanilla and milk.
♦ Beat until smooth. Spread over cake.

Now Let Us Praise Fried Pies

APPLE BROWN BETTY

Apple Brown Betty received its name from Brown Betty who appeared in the Negro minstrel shows that were performed during Christmas in Virginia. Two main characters were Father Christmas and Old Bett or Mother Christmas, who would hand out a dish made from dried apples, molasses and stale bread.

Serves 4

4 apples, cored and thinly sliced	1 tablespoon cinnamon
¼ cup sugar	Juice of ½ lemon
¼ cup brown sugar	¼ cup water
½ stick butter, melted	

- Place water in baking dish. Add apples and sprinkle with lemon juice.
- In a bowl mix together the sugars and cinnamon. Pour over apples, and then butter.
- Bake 350° for ½ hour.
- Serve with vanilla or butter pecan ice cream, or whipped cream.
- ½ cup pecans can be added to the sugar mixture.

SUGAR PLUM CAKE

Yield 6 pounds!!!

1 cup butter	3½ cups flour
2 cups sugar	½ container chopped dates
2 teaspoons lemon juice	1 cup coconut
2 teaspoons vanilla	2 cups pecans
4 eggs	½ pound candied orange
1 teaspoon baking soda	1 pound candied pineapple
1 cup buttermilk	1 pound candied cherries

- Pre heat oven to 250°.
- Chop the orange, pineapple and cherries in small pieces.
- Cream butter and add rest of ingredients, mixing well.
- Place in bundt or large pan and bake for 2 ½ hours.

Now Let Us Praise Fried Pies

OLD FASHIONED FRUIT CAKE

1 pound pecans
1 pound dark raisins
1 8 ounce package figs
1 pound candied cherries
1 8 ounce carton mixed candied
orange and lemon peel
1 tablespoon soda
1½ teaspoons baking powder
1 cup sorghum syrup
1 dozen eggs
1 pound English walnuts

1 pound golden raisins
1 package dates
½ pound candied pineapple
2 cups sugar
6 cups flour
1 cup hot water
1 pound butter
1 tablespoon cinnamon
1 tablespoon nutmeg
1 tablespoon allspice

♦ This recipe makes about 12 pounds of fruitcake.
♦ Mix all fruits and nuts together, dredge with flour.
♦ In another bowl cream sugar and butter. Add eggs and syrup.
♦ Dissolve the soda in hot water and add this alternately with the dry ingredients. Add fruit and nuts.
♦ Grease 6 loaf pans.
♦ Pour batter into pans and bake in pans filled with water.
♦ Bake at 325° for 2 ½ to 3 hours.

Now Let Us Praise Fried Pies

BREAD PUDDING

When we were growing up we frequently had bread pudding for dessert to use up old bread. Today this has become a very popular dish, often made with chocolate, raisins or other ingredients.

2 cups bread cubes (French or
Italian bread)
¼ cup butter, melted
4 cups hot milk

½ cup sugar
2 eggs
1 teaspoon vanilla
½ cup raisins

♦ Preheat oven to 325°.
♦ In a buttered baking dish put in bread, raisins and butter.
♦ Beat together sugar, eggs, milk and vanilla. Pour over bread.
♦ Bake 1 hour. Serve with hard sauce.

HARD SAUCE

½ cup butter, softened
2 cups sugar
1 teaspoon vanilla (rum or bourbon can be substituted)

- ♦ Cream butter and sugar and add vanilla. Refrigerate.
- ♦ Serve over plum pudding or gingerbread.

PLUM PUDDING

The serving of plum pudding dates back to pagan times when the Celtic god, Dagda, lived in Britain. Dagda was the god of plenty. When he saw that the sun had come closer to the earth as the days lengthened he chose to hold a festival. He built a fire and placed a large cauldron on it. Into the pot he put the most delicious fruits of the earth. When he tasted it at the Yuletide, he rejoiced. Today plum pudding is served at Christmas and is dedicated to Christ, who came to "enlighten the world". In England a coin is stirred into the batter. Whoever receives the coin is supposed to have good luck during the coming year.

4 cups bread crumbs
4 cups flour
2 cups sugar
1 teaspoon salt
1 tablespoon cinnamon
1½ teaspoons grated nutmeg
1½ teaspoons ground cloves
¼ teaspoon allspice
2 pounds chopped suet

2 pounds raisins
2 pounds currants
½ pound candied orange peel
½ pound finely cut citron
2 cups chopped apples
12 eggs
Rind and juice of two lemons
½ cup brandy
1 cup cider

- ♦ Combine all ingredients well in a large bowl.
- ♦ Place the batter so that it comes up 2/3 in the bowl.
- ♦ Cover the bowl with buttered muslin tied with a string.
- ♦ Steam the bowl for three hours in a covered pot.
- ♦ This should make 4 fruitcakes.
- ♦ Coffee cans can be substituted for the bowls.
- ♦ Serve with brandy or hard sauce.

BRANDY SAUCE

1 cup sugar
½ cup butter
2 eggs, beaten

1 cup cream
1 teaspoon vanilla
¼ cup brandy

- ◆ Cream together sugar and butter. Add eggs and cream.
- ◆ Cook until slightly thickened, but not boiling. Add vanilla and brandy.
- ◆ Chill.
- ◆ Serve over plum pudding or gingerbread.

LOU'S PLUM PUDDING

1½ cups flour
½ teaspoon baking soda
½ teaspoon salt
½ teaspoon cinnamon
½ teaspoon ground cloves
½ teaspoon allspice

1 cup chopped suet
½ cup apples with skin, chopped
1 cup raisins
½ cup currants
½ cup molasses
½ cup cold water

- ◆ Combine all ingredients in a bowl.
- ◆ Place in a container that fits in a pressure cooker (a coffee can may be used). Cook under pressure for 40 minutes.
- ◆ Cool at once.
- ◆ Serve with hard sauce.

COOKIE MONSTERS

There isn't a child, or an adult who won't like this "low cal" dessert.

Large chocolate chip cookies
Vanilla ice cream
Hot fudge sauce

Whipped cream
Cherries

- ◆ Using the "The Very Best Chocolate Chip Cookie" recipe, make very large 6" diameter or more cookies.
- ◆ Top with vanilla ice cream, hot fudge sauce, whipped cream and a cherry.

SCRIPTURE CAKE

Scripture Cake originated in England, later coming to America. If you drive around the Chesapeake region many of the roads and towns have Biblical names, so it is appropriate to include this cake.

½ cup Judges 5:25, last clause ½ cup butter
2 cups Jeremiah 6:20 2 cups sugar
2 tablespoons I Samuel 14:25 2 tablespoons honey
6 Jeremiah 17:11, separated 6 eggs
1½ cups I Kings 4:22 1½ cups flour
2 teaspoons Amos 4:5 2 teaspoons baking powder
Pinch of Leviticus 2:13 ¼ teaspoon salt
½ cup Judges 4:19 ½ cup milk
2 cups Nahum 3:12, chopped 2 cups figs
2 cups Numbers 17:8 2 cups almonds
2 cups I Samuel 30:12, chopped 2 cups raisins
II Chronicles 9:9 2 teaspoons cinnamon, ½ teaspoon cloves, 1 teaspoon nutmeg, ½ teaspoon ginger

- Preheat the oven to 300°.
- Grease a 10 inch tube pan.
- Whip together the Judges, Jeremiah, and I Samuel until light.
- Beat the 6 egg yolks of Jeremiah 17 and add the Kings, Amos, Chronicles, and Leviticus, alternating with Judges.
- Fold in Nahum, Numbers, and Samuel.
- Beat Jeremiah 17's 6 egg whites until stiff and fold into the rest of the batter.
- Pour into pan and bake 2 hours.

INDEX

217